TWICKENHAM

by the same author

Best Rugby Stories (ed.)
A History of Rugby
The Lions
The Men in White
The Rugby Companion
There Was Also Some Rugby
The Unsmiling Giants
The Winter Men
The World of Rugby

TWICKENHAM

The Story of a Rugby Ground

by

Wallace Reyburn

London
George Allen & Unwin Ltd
Ruskin House Museum Street

First published in 1976

This book is copyright under the Berne Convention. All rights are reserved. Apart from any fair dealing for the purpose of private study, research, criticism or review, as permitted under the Copyright Act, 1956, no part of this publication may be reproduced, stored in a retrieval system, or transmitted, in any form or by any means, electronic, electrical, chemical, mechanical, optical, photocopying, recording or otherwise, without the prior permission of the copyright owner. Enquiries should be addressed to the publishers.

© George Allen & Unwin Ltd 1976

ISBN 0 04 796044 2

Acknowledgements

The author would like to thank the Rugby Football Union for their help and co-operation.

Illustrations are reproduced by permission of the following:

Miller and Harris p. 50
Syndication International p. 87
BBC p. 107
Colorsport pp. 70, 99, 124, 142, 154, 157, 168, 169, 173, 175
Central News p. 41
Press Association pp. 34, 38, 39, 130
Sport and General pp. 13, 47, 48, 52, 55, 58, 68, 77, 81, 84 (top of page), 85, 86 (bottom of page), 91, 92, 95, 108, 114, 116, 121, 126, 129, 133, 139, 140, 144, 149, 156, 158, 163, 166
Aerofilms p. 8

Printed in Great Britain
in 11 point Baskerville
by Cox & Wyman Ltd
London, Fakenham and Reading

Contents

		page
1	Personal Prelude	7
2	The Cabbage Patch	12
3	The International Situation	20
4	The Wakefield Era	32
5	The Brownlie Incident	37
6	The Twickenham Look	46
7	That Immaculate Turf	53
8	The Great Varsity Match	61
9	The Booming Sevens	67
10	Twickenham's Famous Bath Tubs	72
11	A Notable First	76
12	Royal Occasions	83
13	The Link between Rugby and Beer	90
14	When Scotland Did Not Disappoint	98
15	Getting the Picture	104
16	When the War Was Over	113
17	The Notorious Match	118
18	'Anyone Got a Spare Ticket?'	123
19	The Marathon Try	135
20	Twickenham's Round-the-Year Workers	138
21	The Demo Season	146
22	Life in the Press Box	153
23	The Baa-baas Come to Twickenham	159
24	Why Aren't They the Same at Home?	172

Chapter 1

Personal Prelude

Due to circumstances beyond my control, as they say, I lived for fourteen years in Canada. During that time I paid return visits to England but always in the traditional holiday months of summer. So I was somewhat starved, to put it mildly, for rugby.

Then things turned out so that I was able to return to London to live there again. I hung up my rarely used Toronto club jersey and took ship to England. I arrived in London on a Friday in February and although I had many pressing things to do I cast them aside for the nonce and bought an evening paper at the bookstall in the hotel lobby. What was on at Twickenham tomorrow? – that was the important thing!

It turned out to be one of the Inter-Services matches and on a cold, bleak day it was poorly attended. But that did not matter. I can still vividly remember arriving at the ground that day and taking my place in a very good seat indeed among the modest cluster of devotees in the West Stand. Whether the Army beat the RAF on that occasion (or was it the Navy versus the Army?) I cannot recall. Sufficient to be at Twickenham again after such a long lay-off.

Even better, though, was to arrive in time to get a ticket a couple of weeks later for England's next International. Regulars at Twickenham feel an upsurge of excitement every time they go to an International there; you can imagine how exhilarating it was for me, and always is for the returned exile, to be caught up again in the special atmosphere of the big match at what used to be called Twickers. Not without good reason is the commonest bit of special pleading by those who phone the ground trying to get a ticket for a sold-out match: 'I've been abroad for years and have just got back. I *must* see an International again.'

What is that special atmosphere of Twickenham that those at home so much enjoy and those exiled abroad pine for?

Regulars at Twickenham might well be called Twickhamists and

Twickenham today. This side of River Crane running across foreground are playing fields of a primary school. The West Car Park (right), with the North and East, accommodate 3,000 vehicles. Whitton Road, leading to the station, is at roundabout (top).

Personal Prelude 9

divide themselves into two basic types – the ones who come by car and those who come by train. The former are very much inclined to have pre-match picnics in the car parks, the West Car Park undoubtedly being the Ritz of the Twickenham picnic grounds. It is quite a vista – those hundreds of cars with their gaping open boots at the back, each a cornucopia of good things to eat and drink. Nothing on the level of a choice of polythene-wrapped cheese or ham sandwiches accompanied by beer or a can of 'Coke', these are sumptuous repasts, unloaded from the picnic hampers in the boot and laid out on trestle tables – chicken legs, pâté, Quiche Lorraine, potato salad, lettuce salad, French bread, Danish Blue, Stilton, trifle, fruit, with gin-and-tonic and gin-and-French and Scotch for starters, through the appropriate wines to liqueurs. I remember before one England–Wales match in a season when nobody had any great hopes for England I came upon a Dormobile beside which two trestle tables end to end were needed to accommodate the vast array of food and drink, and as I stood there gazing at what looked like a fork luncheon at Claridge's, one of the cluster of gentlemen tucking in smiled and said: 'We call it the last supper.'

These are the *crème de la crème* of the Twickhamists. They emerge from the West Car Park well before the kick-off, to allow time for chatting in the West Concourse, described as 'one of the world's most famous meeting places'. They used to be called the British Warm Brigade, because father always wore the British Warm from his days at the Front in the Great War. Now perhaps it would be more accurate to call them the Sheepskin Car-coat Crowd. Mother, however, has remained steadfastly consistent in her attire, for she is still relentlessly tweedy, with the steamer rug over her arm for tucking snugly around the knees in the West Stand. The boy with his exeat from school is along with them, standing there self-consciously as his parents chat with their middle-aged friends, one of whom will take pity on him and enquire: 'Well, Simon, how are you enjoying Haileybury?'

The whole scene is well up the social ladder from those whose meeting place is 'See you at the railings outside the turnstile entrance'. These represent the other basic category of Twickhamists – the ones who come by train. They are a much younger set and come by train not necessarily because they do not run a car. They are probably recovering from a Friday night party, have just managed to get through their Saturday morning hung-over club match and have a heavy day's drinking ahead of them.

One could call them the Field Ticket Crowd, or the Scruffy Mob. They are at great pains to look untidy, with their long hair, their afghans and donkey jackets and their cords and denim flares – all the gear mellowed with age. It is a studied avoidance of looking well groomed, the casual look carried to its ultimate, in drastic contrast to their forerunners of the 1930s, with their shiny Brylcreemed hair beneath their green pork-pie hats, in their bum-freezer jackets and Daks flannels, all dressed up like a well-kept grave.

The interesting thing is that the Scruffy Mob are the same young men as their predecessors – the true fabric of rugby support, the younger generation who love the game and who, when they marry the girls who are along with them and have youngsters, will put an oval ball into their hands as soon as they can walk.

With the general rugby public they emerge from Twickenham railway station into the Whitton Road, that well-known walk to the ground, along which at midday there is a trickle of people, which swells to a stream and then to a veritable flood as kick-off time approaches. In places the Whitton Road narrows to a mere fourteen yards across, and the Twickenham fans, shoulder-to-shoulder, take over the whole street – roadway and footpaths – so that any motorist who tries to make his way along it at that time is either foolhardy or ignorant of what happens there on a big-match day.

One is caught up in the sights and the sounds, not to mention the smells – the stench from the hotdog stands strangely belying the products they sell, since they are found to be quite palatable on purchase.

The ticket spivs are there – 'Anyone want tickets for the match?' – fanning out an array of pasteboards like a good poker hand. 'Ten quid, best seat in the ground . . . hey, come back, what yer want to pay?' And any genuine rugby fan who happens to have a spare ticket will take delight in offering it at face value to the ticketless one right beside the spivs, for the joy of hearing them let out a torrent of abuse – but not too loud, because of the coppers nearby.

Young men out in the street hopefully wave motorists in the direction of private parking space in front of houses set well back from the road. 'Car Park – 40p – Near all the Pubs and the Ground', the notice says.

Householders come out and ask, 'What time will the game be over today?', so that they can be prepared for the reverse flood of fans after the final whistle.

The rosette sellers are there hawking the results of their wives' and daughters' labours at the sewing machine. From their ribbons of white, red, blue, green, yellow and black, you can perm the colours of any major International team. Up the road are the sellers of phoney programmes, about as accurate and informative as books on *Your Dreams Interpreted*.

A Welshman will tell you that at Twickenham there is nothing like the pre-match atmosphere inside the ground that there is at Cardiff

Arms Park, or the National Stadium, as they are trying to make us call it. 'Ah, the singing', he will say. Of course they sing at the Arms Park before a match, because they've got nothing else to do there. No restaurants, no car park picnics. They're not allowed to buy a drink. At Twickenham they are too busy having friendly get-togethers while chewing on chicken legs or in the bars to go up into the stands and terraces and sing.

The singing comes later, when the match is over and they flock back into the bars to hold liquid post-mortems on the game and then burst into songs which may not be quite as uplifting as Welsh hymns but are just as lustily delivered.

Chapter 2

The Cabbage Patch

The Rugby Football Union came into being at a meeting in a London restaurant in 1871. By the turn of the century it had its headquarters in an unpretentious suite of offices in Surrey Street, across the Strand from what is now Australia House.

When its chosen England side undertook fixtures against visiting sides from the other Home Countries – and, starting in 1905, from the Dominions and France – the matches were played at a variety of venues all around the country. The very first home Internationals were played in the shadow of the gasometers at the Oval cricket ground in Kennington; thereafter this was the order in which the other venues came on to the rota: Manchester, Blackheath, Richmond, Leeds, Dewsbury, Birkenhead, Bristol, Gloucester, Leicester and Crystal Palace.

By the early 1900s the meagre accommodation at Surrey Street was no longer adequate to support the increasing responsibilities of the Rugby Union, and this, together with the complications of staging Internationals and other big matches without a ground of its own, made RFU officials and others who had the development of the game at heart realise that the time had come for expansion. One man who felt very keenly about this was Billy Williams, then in his forties but still a prominent sporting figure, and it was mainly through his efforts that Twickenham became automatically linked in the minds of people all over the world with sport in the same way as Wimbledon, Wembley, Ascot and Henley.

As a player Billy Williams was much better known as a cricketer than in rugby. He played rugby for his school, Buxdon College, Essex, and had some games for Harlequins as an honorary member but in cricket his career was remarkable. He played wicket-keeper for Middlesex from 1885 until 1887 and then switched to leg-break bowling, at which he was a regular for the MCC, touring with them under the captaincy of A. Priestley to the West Indies in the 1896–7 season. By then thirty-seven years of age it was not until another thirty-seven

W. (Billy) Williams, RFU Committee member 1904–25, who found the 'cabbage patch' in Twickenham which was to become the site for the rugby ground.

years had elapsed that, at seventy-four, he decided the time had come for him to retire. Even at that age it had not been as a 'passenger' that he turned out for his club. In his fifty-five years with them he never failed to get his hundred wickets in a season.

On the rugby field he had been best known for his refereeing, since he was at the centre of a controversy that arose with regard to New Zealand's detached wing-forward or 'rover'. When the 1905 All Blacks came on tour, their captain, Dave Gallaher, was the chief performer in this role and the British press, particularly the London papers, railed against this 'cheat' who put the ball in the scrum and was close at hand to harass the opposing scrum-half, although there was nothing in the laws of the game then forbidding it. The criticisms were so scorching that when those first All Blacks came to London to play Surrey half way through the tour, Gallaher felt it prudent to stand down and the spare full-back, Gillett, was seconded to the rover position. S. F. Start, who was later to be capped for England at scrum-half, was the recipient of the rover's attentions on this occasion and referee Billy Williams left no doubt in anyone's mind as to how he felt about the New Zealanders' detached wing-forward ploy. By half-time he had awarded twelve penalties against Gillett and this, coupled with further brisk whistling-up in the second half, was a contributing factor to the All Blacks' 11–0 defeat of Surrey being the smallest winning margin of their nineteen unbeaten games in England.

In recognition of what he had done towards providing rugby with a headquarters to be proud of, Billy Williams was elected Vice-President of the Rugby Football Union in 1924–5. Born in 1860 he died at the ripe old age of ninety-one, which meant that he was to see more than forty years of the development of his brainchild.

It had been in 1907, after more than a year of scouting around for possible sites, that Billy Williams decided that a stretch of land partially in use as a market garden on the outskirts of the then small community of Twickenham would be an ideal location. But when he put the idea up to the RFU he at once met with opposition. One objection was that the area was subject to flooding from the nearby River Crane, a tributary of the Thames, but the main argument against it brought up by members of the committee was its remoteness.

Granted there was a railway link with Twickenham but to go by other means was not, as today, merely a drive across London to its outskirts; it was a twelve-mile journey right out into the country. To set up a rugby ground and Rugby Union offices there was criticised as being 'fearsomely remote from Piccadilly Circus'. But one argument put forward by Billy Williams and those who supported him was that Kneller Hall was already established within a stone's throw of the site he had in mind and if, for half a century, military bandsmen and bandmasters had been coming and going from there without a feeling of remoteness, surely rugbymen could do the same. He won the day. The decision was made to go ahead and £5,572 12s 6d was paid for ten and a quarter acres of land which became known in the rugby world as 'Billy Williams's cabbage patch'.

Since the River Crane, also alluded to from time to time as the Duke of Northumberland's River and Birkett's Brook, was regarded as a flooding menace, its banks were built up and fortified with concrete and it became the 20-foot wide irrigation ditch we know today. Its only serious attempt to render the Twickenham pitch unplayable was in 1927 when it flooded the West Car Park, which ruled out picnic lunches but never interrupted play.

The stretch of flat horticultural land purchased in 1907 did not adjoin the Whitton Road. The row of houses which stand between the roadway and the ground itself, with entrance alleyways in between, were in existence at the time of the purchase. In some ways it was a pity they were there, since if that land had been vacant it would have been possible to have a more imposing entrance approach to the ground. However, over the years it has been possible for the RFU to buy them all, which has proved a satisfactory arrangement since these and other houses further along the road now provide living accommodation for those permanently employed at Twickenham.

No sooner had the 'cabbage patch' been made over to its new owners than work was started on what was hoped would be a worthy headquarters for the Rugby Football Union. The minutes of the annual general meeting of 1908 showed that in the first year of construction £1,606 9s 4d had been expended on all sorts of things from architects' fees to the actual laying of the pitch. The latter, in view of all the worry about flooding, involved an elaborate system of drainage and, although we probably do not realise it when we go to Twickenham today, the playing surface is set above the level of the surrounding land.

More than £8,000 was spent on the second year's work – including the building of roads and entrances, mounds and terraces, and a cottage for the groundsman – and by 1909, with the further expenditure of some £20,000, Twickenham Rugby Football Ground was ready for business.

This original version consisted of two single-deck covered stands along each touchline, called at first 'A' and 'B' but soon to be referred to as the West and East. Each had 3,000 seats. Open terracing at the southern end could accommodate 7,000 people, and space for a further 17,000 standing spectators in front of the stands and on the mound at the northern end gave the ground a possible capacity of 30,000. Space for conveyances – horse-drawn or motorised – which carried spectators to the match was limited to 200 at the rear of the South Terrace, since the purchase of additional land for parking facilities, which brought the property to its present thirty acres, was some time away.

At the planning stage there had been talk of making Twickenham an oval, since a bigger perimeter would make for larger spectator accommodation, but in the end the planners settled for simply following the rectangular shape of the pitch, the covered stands being slightly concave so that those watching from each end could see along the near touchline.

We can be thankful today that those in favour of an oval were talked out of it, for the whole development of Twickenham to its modern 72,500 capacity has perforce been based on that original layout. It is this that has given the ground its essential character of steeply rising double-decker stands and the feeling of intimacy between the onlookers and what is happening on the field.

We are fortunate, too, that the Rugby Union from the outset chose its architects at Twickenham wisely, something which cannot be said for all sports bodies. One wonders, for example, what the MCC of yesteryear were about when they inflicted upon spectators at Lord's that elongated dungeon under the Father Time grandstand, which is only slightly less depressing than the accommodation under what used to be known as the Free Seats at the nursery end of the ground.

WHAT THE PAPERS SAID

The first-ever match played at Twickenham was on Saturday, 2 October 1909, but all *The Times* carried about it was this simple entry in the list of the day's rugby fixtures:

> Harlequins *v.* Richmond (Twickenham)

Even in the Monday issue, where there might have been more generous coverage of the historical event, there was only:

FOOTBALL
Rugby Union Rules
Harlequins v. Richmond

> The match between these two clubs attracted some 3,000 spectators to the new Rugby ground at Twickenham which the Harlequins have secured for their home matches. The South-Western Railway are arranging a special service of trains and thus the ground is easily accessible. The new stands are excellent structures and the enclosure should become popular. The grass has been kept very long, as compared with other ground, in order to protect the young turf, which has to last through a long season.

This was followed by a brief account of the match itself 'won by Harlequins by one goal and 3 tries to two goals largely due to the excellent judgment and understanding that existed between A. D. Stoop and J. G. G. Birkett'.

That was all. A mere $3\frac{1}{2}$ column inches, vastly outweighed by a

The first ever match at Twickenham, between Harlequins and Richmond in 1909. Hands on knees (left) is Ronnie Poulton-Palmer.

15-inch story next door to it on the 'Opening of the Lacrosse Season at Lord's'.

One could have hoped for more sense of occasion but no doubt that was to come when Twickenham was properly unveiled as England's national rugby stadium, three months later when the first International took place there. However, the Monday *Times* after Twickenham's first International on 15 January 1910 only had this somewhat complaining paragraph about the ground itself:

'The stands and general arrangements on the Twickenham ground itself are excellent, but the entrances and exits from the ground are open to considerable improvement. There was quite a nasty crush at the Whitton-road exit at the end of the game. And at least half an hour elapsed before any of the motor-cars or cabs were allowed to proceed on their way to the ground. The approach to the Whitton-road end of the ground is shaped somewhat like the neck of a bottle and other means will have to be found before the next International match for dealing with the big crowds which nowadays patronise these matches. There must have been 20,000 spectators on Saturday.'

In the hope of finding something more rewarding by way of contemporary comment on the unveiling of Twickenham, I looked up the files of the two weekly local papers.

The *Thames Valley Times* of 6 October 1909:

> 'The new Rugby Union ground at Twickenham was opened on Saturday with a game between Harlequin F.C., who are the occupants of the ground for the season, and Richmond. There was no formal opening ceremony, but the 3,500 people or so present saw what was to them perhaps more interesting than this, a keen game of Rugby football . . . That the ground and its appointments are good one must admit. The hypercritical will doubtless find some points to grumble about – if it pleased all it would be a marvellous ground.
>
> 'Whether it was wanted or not is not a question to go into here. It has been established and it is for the Rugby Union itself to make it pay without – and this is a very important point – doing any injury to any of the grounds of the metropolitan clubs who, be it remembered, have largely helped in the accumulation of the funds which have made the establishment of the new ground possible.
>
> 'On Saturday the grass was a little too long for fast football, but surely Mr Marriott, the conscientious secretary and manager of the ground, will put this right by next Saturday.
>
> 'One objection to the ground has been its distance from the station. One scribe said it took him twelve minutes to do the walk. All we can say is that he would stand a poor chance in the "Marathon". To the Oak Lane entrance the walk should not occupy more than eight minutes and surely that is not much. On Saturday the London and South Western Railway Company, rising to the occasion, put on a special train which did the journey from Waterloo in 22 minutes, so that anyone who came by that must have been on the ground in about half an hour. That very few of the spectators objected to the walk is proved by the fact that a large brake in readiness to convey passengers from the Railway Station to the ground at the small charge of 3d didn't do a single outward journey.'

The *Richmond and Twickenham Times* of 9 October 1909 on the opening of the ground:

> 'Opinions as to the ground itself seem to be somewhat divided, but the general impression certainly seems to be in its favour. It is of vast proportions but the public are not so far from the players as at first would seem to be the case and a good view of the game is to be obtained from any part of the ground. It would have been

better if the grass had been mown on Saturday, it is true, but I think that some of my fellow scribes make too much of that fact. As to the distance from the railway station, that should mean little to Rugby enthusiasts, though it may be a little uncomfortable on wet days.'

After all the work they had put into converting a cabbage patch into the most up-to-date rugby ground of its time, Billy Williams and his associates could hardly have been very excited about those rather bare reports.

Chapter 3

The International Situation

In the special souvenir programme brought out for the Twickenham Jubilee Match between England-and-Wales and Scotland-and-Ireland on 17 October 1959 there were reminiscences by D. R. Gent which included an account of the 15 January 1910 game, in which he played scrum-half for England.

'Dai' Gent was born in 1883 and went to St Paul's Training College in Cheltenham before becoming a teacher in various schools, in Gloucester, Saltash, Maidstone and Eastbourne, and then rugby correspondent for *The Sunday Times*. He became the respected and much loved doyen of the press box, raised many schoolboy and senior sides and was the author of several coaching books on the game. He died in 1964.

This reminiscence is not just the bare-bones account of a match but captures the mood of rugby as it was played in those days.

TWICKENHAM'S FIRST INTERNATIONAL
England v. Wales, 15 January 1910

'Is it really fifty years since the first International match was played on the Twickenham Ground? To those of us who took part in it and are still able to follow the game, it seems at times but yesterday that we walked off the field after winning a wonderful match. In my case, the thrill largely lay in the fact that here was the new Home Ground of Rugby Football, that I had played on it, for the first time, and that, wonder of wonders, we had beaten Wales for the first time since 1898.

'It so happened that I had played for England before, in the season 1905–6, against the magnificent original "All Blacks", against Wales and against Ireland. But there was no Rugby "Home" then and these three matches were played at the Crystal Palace (the largest suitable ground we could find), on the homely Richmond Athletic Ground, Leicester, and other Rugby Grounds used were Gloucester (my home ground), Bristol, Manchester, Blackheath and a few others. What tales the veterans of those days could tell of the so-called "amenities" provided on or off the ground for the players, and I could join in with a few!

'Well, the great game of Rugby Union Football had at last found its Home and a new name was added to Rugby Football – Twickenham! Since the third Saturday in January 1910, England has played all her home matches on this ground and thanks to the energy, imagination, enthusiasm and courage of all connected with the Union (and that includes Presidents, Committeemen, officials, players and hundreds of enthusiasts by their gifts and support in all sorts of ways) their efforts have provided a superb playing pitch, increasingly adequate modern standards and all the other additions and facilities to accommodate at least 73,000 spectators, with more to come, I'm sure. So here's to "Twickenham", without doubt the loveliest of Rugby Grounds, today celebrating its 50th season, with still a few of us left to join in the festivities as we did 50 years ago.

'Now to the epoch-making first match itself. Gloucester was my club (and a great club, too!) and I felt more than a little tired after the Christmas of 1909, during which we had played the usual three matches in four days. So I had asked my captain (A. Hudson, an international wing threequarter and in every way a splendid player and still at 76 secretary of the Gloucester club!) to let me have a rest for the coming Saturday. On the Tuesday I received a wire from Charles Marriott, the R.U. Secretary and a great character, inviting me to play for the Rest against England, as the chosen scrum-half had withdrawn. I still really felt sore after the buffeting of the previous few days and as I had had three "caps" in the 1905-6 season, still seriously thought of refusing the offer. One thing made me decide to accept it. During the seasons 1906-9 we in the Provinces, old clubs like Leicester, Gloucester, Devon Albion and Bristol, felt that the Harlequins were having rather too much Press publicity, and the Provincial sides far too little. Adrian Stoop and his "brilliant backs" were having a great time of it in all the papers. I looked again at the two Final Trial sides and though I knew a few of the "England" side (R. W. Poulton, J. G. Birkett, F. M. Stoop, A. D. Stoop and H. J. Sibree were their backs), I did know all the Rest men well, for most of them were Provincials whom I had met many times in club or county football, and I knew them to be really good players. I thought I'd love to have a go at these Harlequins backs, led by Adrian Stoop (F.M. was his younger brother) and after some consideration I accepted!

'When I got to this new Ground in embryo, but not yet officially opened, I had a look at the players. I found that I was partnered with Harry Coverdale, a very good player indeed. He afterwards became an England Selector and was during his playing days one of the best players in the then strong Durham side, coming South later on to play for Blackheath. I captained the Rest – a really first class English side, and we all played our best. We had more of the ball perhaps than Stoop's side and his own backs were at sixes and sevens, with the result that at half time these "World Beaters" were about a dozen points behind! The Selectors changed me over at half time to play with Stoop, and two of the Rest threequarters, F. E. Chapman (he it was who scored the first try in the Welsh match a fortnight later) and B. Solomon, who also scored a try in the Welsh match, joined me.

'That was my first appearance with one of the real geniuses of the Rugby game . . . He and I had a word or two about tactics just before the re-start and then it was "Off!" I never played with a smoother partner and the new "England" side played very much better. The three of us that "went over" at half time were in the new England side to play Wales a fortnight later – the day of the first Twickenham International. . . .

'The teams were:

'*England:* W. R. Johnston (Bristol); F. E. Chapman (W. Hartlepool), J. G. G. Birkett (Harlequins), B. Solomon (Redruth), R. W. Poulton-Palmer (Oxford); A. D. Stoop (Harlequins, capt.), D. R. Gent (Gloucester); C. H. Pillman (Blackheath), E. L. Chambers (Cambridge), H. Berry (Gloucester), L. Haigh (Manchester), D. F. Smith (Richmond), W. A. Johns (Gloucester), H. J. S. Morton (Cambridge), L. E. Barrington-Ward (Edinburgh U).

'*Wales:* J. Bancroft (Swansea); W. J. Trew (Swansea, capt.), J. P. Jones (Pontypool), P. Hopkins (Swansea), R. Gibbs (Cardiff); R. Jones (Swansea), R. M. Owen (Swansea); B. Gronow (Bridgend), C. M. Pritchard (Newport), J. Pugsley (Cardiff), T. Evans (Llanelli), J. Webb (Abertillery), H. Jarman (Newport), D. J. Thomas (Swansea), Ivor Morgan (Swansea).

'Referee: J. D. Dallas (Scotland).

'The really great days of Welsh football were over round about this period, though J. Bancroft (younger brother of W. J. Bancroft, one of the greatest of all full-backs), W. J. Trew, R. M. Owen and Ivor Morgan were of the highest class, with Trew the finest player I have ever seen, fit to take any position behind the scrum. I played against or with him as wing threequarter, centre or outside half.

'It was a damp, raw day when we took the field, a quarter of an hour late, it so happened, and, incidentally, in the confusion there was no team photo taken. Stoop chose to play defending the South end, having won the toss, though there was little in the weather conditions either way. In a couple of minutes after the kick off this historic match was won by England! Wales kicked off and both sides had aligned themselves in the usual manner, England filling up their half of the field and the Welshmen gathering on either side of the kicker and a little behind him. The opening gambit was, as usual in those days, for the side that kicked off to kick up and across the field and for their forwards to follow up and prevent a clean return to touch, where the game generally really started.

'But Stoop had other ideas for this match, and the Welshmen just played into his hands. He had taken his position about midway between the goal-line and halfway line. The ball came straight to him and, as ever, he fielded it cleanly. But then—! Instead of kicking he started to run at once, at top speed, up the field and diagonally towards the left. Though surprised, we all quickly tumbled to what he was doing and moved up on his inside. Outside him he had Solomon, Birkett and Poulton, and the ball was passed along the line at top speed. When it reached Poulton on the left wing he was hemmed in and wisely put in a cross kick that dropped in front of the posts. Once more we started passing (they say it was I who picked the ball up), this time along the line towards Chapman on our right wing, and in a flash Chapman was over in the north-eastern or right hand corner – as good a try as one would ever wish to see. The Welshmen were caught napping, as most sides would have been, and Chapman, to add to our joy, converted with a beautiful shot, so that in less than a couple of minutes we were five points up.

'This was indeed the right way to open a new Ground! The England supporters yelled with delight and they kept this up for the rest of the match. (There was an attendance of about 18,000.) We pressed for all we were worth and kept our opponents very much on edge, and especially Owen and Morgan (the Welsh wing forward) who found it very difficult to make headway against Charles Pillman and myself, he on one side of the scrum and myself on the other. We kept up the pressure and Chapman kicked a penalty goal for us. At once Wales responded, this time with a try from T. Evans, a forward, but Bancroft failed with the kick. Again we fought back and scored a beautiful try. A passing movement along the line reached Solomon with Chapman on his right. Solomon feinted brilliantly, his opponents all going for his right wing, and the Cornishman doubled back inside to score between the posts. That made the half time score 11 points to 3 in our favour, for this easy shot at goal was missed.

'We found the second half heavy going. Our opponents were

getting well under way and Trew and Owen and Ivor Morgan took a lot of stopping. They scored once, a clever move by Trew, Owen and Gibbs clean beating our defence, and Gibbs scoring a try. The kick was missed but we hung on like grim death and we won, deservedly, the opening match at Twickenham by a goal, a penalty goal and a try to two tries.

'I have said enough about this particular match already, I'm afraid. But it was truly a great occasion and did bring English Rugby Union Football and its new Home straight away into the limelight. I will just add the names of a few players who did particularly well. These were Stoop himself; Johnston our full-back; Birkett; Berry (a grand forward from my own club, who was killed in the 1914–1918 War) and Charles Pillman, the old Tonbridge boy. The delightful and cheery and skilful Pillman became a superb wing forward (at School he had often been an outside half). It was a joy to play with him in the opening match and many other matches as I did, with him or against him. Johnston became a great full-back – a good sense of position, a beautiful fielder of the ball, a wonderful tackler, and always revelling in stopping rushes. He played in nearly all the England matches from 1910–1914.

'I must just add this! I was captain of Gloucestershire in the 1909–10 season and for the first time in the County's history we won the Championship, and we had six English Internationals in the Gloucestershire side, a lot for a Provincial county in one season: W. R. Johnston, W. A. Johns, A. Hudson, H. Berry, L. W. Hayward and myself. I was indeed a proud person, leading the Champion County and playing in the opening match at Twickenham!'

Another interesting aspect of the winter of 1909–10, Twickenham's first season, was that it saw the arrival on the rugby scene of something else of great importance. It was the first season of the Five Nations Championship.

British rugby fans take it for granted now that there are two Internationals on their home ground each year, and the bonus of a third when a major touring side is visiting. But it was not like that for our grandfathers when they were young. With France not a fully fledged member of the International circuit, the British rugby enthusiasts could look forward merely to one Home International and two away, alternating season by season.

England supporters were the first to get two regular Internationals at home each season, in 1906 when their Rugby Union came to what might be termed a unilateral agreement with France to play home and away fixtures. The Welsh acknowledged France in 1908 and the Irish did likewise in 1909.

Scotland, traditionally the most reactionary and slow-moving of the Home Unions, found themselves left out in the cold, with England, Wales and Ireland each enjoying four Internationals each season and the Scots only three. So they climbed on the bandwagon, inviting France to join their fixture list in 1910, and in that way the Five Nations Championship came into being, the home-and-away sequence of playing matches remaining precisely the same today as when it started that year. As far as England is concerned it is Wales and Ireland at Twickenham one season and Scotland and France the next.

In the first five years of Twickenham's history, brought to a close by the outbreak of the 1914–18 war, the spectators who came in new-fangled motor cars, scaring the horses as they stuttered by, and who came in the steam trains from Waterloo at 1s 2d third-class return, were attracted mainly by the prospect of seeing in action England's brilliant backs of that period.

However, there was at least one forward who was a great crowd-pleaser, in the person of C. H. 'Cherry' Pillman. He had watched the 1905 All Black tourists when a Tonbridge schoolboy and been fascinated by their seven-man scrum and detached forward, whose roving role he tried to emulate when he played for Blackheath and eventually for England. Within the limitations of having to pack down in the scrum – unlike the New Zealand 'rover', who put the ball in the scrum, among other back-type activities – Pillman played the same sort of game as he had seen New Zealand's captain, Dave Gallaher, play. As a spoiler of opponents' possession from set pieces and a link with his own inside backs on attack, Pillman was a pioneer of the No. 8 as we know him today. He made his debut for England, as a 19-year-old, in that first-ever International at Twickenham against Wales, and his entire, curtailed playing career for the national side, eighteen caps in all, was encompassed by that five-year period prior to Twickenham being given over as a wartime grazing ground for horses.

But Pillman excepted, what the crowds flocked to Twickenham to see were England's great 'outsides', as backs used to be called in those days.

The state of rugby as a whole at that time should be borne in mind. It was only at the turn of the century that rugby emerged from being a predominantly forward, mauling game. With their introduction in 1893 of the four three-quarter system the Welsh had put more accent on the back divisions and in 1900 entered a golden era in which half-backs and three-quarters such as Dickie Owen, Gwynn Nicholls,

Willie Llewellyn (one could list a dozen really great Welsh backs of that period) were the dominant force behind their being practically unbeatable for a whole decade. Scotland, however, were still relying in the main on their slogging forwards – 'Feet! Feet! Feet!' – and Ireland could always be relied upon to start each match with a pack described as 'fiery', the fire unfortunately having the tendency to flicker and die out after, for example, a sustained session of chasing Wales's dazzling backs around the field.

England, for her part, was taking a very long time to recover from the breakaway of the Northern Union, which oddly enough had been in the very same year that Wales had set herself off on her own thriving course by developing the four three-quarter system. Such damage had the split done to English rugby that in Wales it would have been the equivalent of drawing a line down the middle of South Wales and saying that henceforth only two of the country's four great rugby centres – Cardiff, Newport, Swansea and Llanelli – would remain in the Rugby Union code. Neither in respect of forwards nor backs did England have the reserves of talent to draw on to keep them on anything like the same level as the other Home Unions, until the man who can only be called the saviour came along.

England's resurgence could just as well have been based on forward strength, as was the case when Wakefield & Co. took her to the heights in the 1920s, but it just so happened that Adrian Stoop was a back and not a forward.

It was indeed fortunate for England that Stoop, who was born in 1883, was not merely a player with a good idea of back play. An Old Rugbeian, when he came down from Oxford and joined Harlequins in 1905 he was seen to be a great thinker about the game, a master tactician. It was under his guidance that Harlequins became the great club it was and still shows signs of being. He got his first cap for England in the same year he started with Harlequins and by 1912 had finished with fifteen. His influence on English rugby and on the game as a whole was tremendous.

When he came on the scene back play was not the highly organised operation it is today, specialisation being in its infancy and to a degree actually frowned upon. This applied particularly in the case of half-backs.

Dai Gent once recalled his first match for Gloucestershire early in the century. His partner, W. V. Butcher, of Streatham, was an older player, already capped for England and when they took the field he asked Gent, 'Which side of the field do you like to play on?' Gent did not understand what he was talking about and told him so. It turned out that the reason for confusion was that Gent had learned his rugby in Wales, where it had become the vogue for one half-back to 'work the scrummage' and the other to 'stand-off' as a link with the three-quarters. Gent regarded himself as what was becoming known as a 'scrum-half' and Butcher had to explain that he was accustomed to the system whereby the 'left half-back' worked the scrummage on his side of the field and the 'right half-back' did the chores on the other. However, he let the new boy play the game he was used to.

In his first England Trial, Gent found that his partner, R. A. Jago, of Devonport Albion, was not as accommodating. The captain was brought in as mediator and it was decided that Jago would be scrum-half and Gent stand-off in the first half and then they would switch for the remainder of the game. But then at half-time Jago said that it was working so well that it would be foolish to change over! In point of fact it was at stand-off that Gent, a natural scrum-half in build and temperament, played in his first three England matches in 1906, not being in his rightful spot in the national side until partnered by Adrian Stoop in that historic first International against Wales at Twickenham in 1910.

By then Stoop had, by example, developed the stand-off into a specialised position – the key man in the backs from whom all the tactics stemmed. And the tactics he had evolved were for that period unorthodox. He broke with the convention of just sending the ball out along the back line, with the three-quarters invariably not even drawing their opposing number before passing – the theory was to get the ball out as quickly as possible to your wing, who would be the one to do the scoring. Reasoning quite correctly that often as not this could do nothing but result in congestion on the touchline, with both sets of backs converging in that direction, he placed great stress on change of direction, the reverse pass, the cross-kick. The aimless handling of the ball on by one back to another was something he could not abide. He wrote an essay on passing and its importance, the drawing of opponents, getting the ball to one's team mate so that he can take it easily on the burst, which today is still a valuable read for anyone embarking on rugby.

At Harlequins to carry out his ideas with him Stoop had J. G. G. Birkett and Ronnie Poulton-Palmer as centres and this mid-field trio, who carried out their moves like a well-oiled machine, operated together for England, with C. N. ('Kid') Lowe, of Blackheath, coming in later on the wing to provide the Twickenham crowds with the scintillating sort of back play to which England supporters had not previously been accustomed.

Birkett was the son of an International, R. H. Birkett, and had an uncle, Louis, who also was capped. Birkett's father had the rare distinction, shared only by C. P. Wilson and J. W. Sutcliffe, of playing for England at both rugby and soccer. Birkett himself was to feature in the record books – as scorer of the first-ever try at Twickenham, for Harlequins in the inaugural match against Richmond in 1909, and then in 1912 when he retired as England's leading cap winner with twenty-one, a record not broken until 1923, by Lowe with twenty-five.

Stoop, as England's captain and master tactician, was naturally greatly admired but if the fans at Twickenham in that first truncated decade of its history had an idol it was Poulton-Palmer, the handsome, spectacular three-quarter who scored five tries for Oxford in the Varsity Match of 1909, the year of his debut for England – a record that still stands.

Although equally at home on the wing, there seems no question that Poulton-Palmer was the greatest centre England has produced. I say this not merely judging from contemporary reports, which can become legendary but not necessarily accurate in the light of events and personalities that follow in the years after a great player is no longer on the scene. W. J. A. Davies, who was fly-half with him in the England sides of the 1913 and 1914 International seasons, died as recently as 1967, so he had opportunities for over half a century of watching the England centres who came after. When I was writing *The World of Rugby* in 1966 I interviewed 'Dave' Davies and mentioned Poulton-Palmer. His eyes lit up. 'There's nobody to compare to him today', he said. 'I've never seen a centre since who could match him. And also he was such a wonderful person, probably the greatest figure that ever played rugby football.'

The charm of young Poulton-Palmer was something mentioned by all his contemporaries. On and off the field he had charisma long before that ever became a vogue word. When he joined the Royal Berkshire Regiment at the outbreak of war and went to the Front in Belgium the men in his company idolised the 25-year-old lieutenant. They were in tears at the dawn stand-to after he had been killed outright in a trench by a sniper's bullet.

The great set of backs England produced in those first Internationals at Twickenham under the inspiration of Adrian Stoop were, however, to learn the truth of the adage that was to apply for many years to the Home Countries when pitted against the giants of South Africa and New Zealand on tour – no matter how brilliant or sophisticated back play may be, it will lose out against forward power. And after being unbeaten at Twickenham in the first three seasons of its being their home ground, England then came up against Billy Millar's 1912–13 Springboks.

ENGLAND v. SOUTH AFRICA
4 January 1913

The teams:

England: W. R. Johnston (Bristol); C. N. Lowe (Cambridge), F. M. Stoop (Harlequins), R. W. Poulton-Palmer (Harlequins), V. H. M. Coates (Bath); W. J. A. Davies (RN and United Services), W. I. Cheesman (OMTS); N. A. Wodehouse (RN and United Services), J. A. King (Headingley), C. H. Pillman (Blackheath), J. E. Greenwood (Cambridge), L. G. Brown (Oxford), A. L. Kewney (Leicester), S. Smart (Gloucester), J. A. Ritson (Northern).

South Africa: P. G. Morkel; J. A. Stegmann, R. R. Luyt, J. W. H. Morkel, E. E. McHardy; F. P. Luyt, J. D. McCulloch; D. F. T. Morkel, T. Van Vuuren, A. S. Knight, J. A. J. Francis, J. D. Luyt, S. H. Ledger, E. H. Shum, W. H. Morkel.

Referee: J. Tulloch (Scotland).

The then record crowd of 29,000 had barely settled into their places in the single-deck West and East stands and on the North and South terraces when Poulton-Palmer started displaying his brilliance. Receiving the ball at outside centre in a conventional back movement he turned in to beat his opposite number, then swerved around the wing coming in to cover and then around the full-back. It was a wonderful solo effort and even more creditable because this try gained the first points to be scored against the tourists in their Internationals, since they had already disposed of Scotland, Ireland and Wales with an aggregate of 57–0.

Three–nil down in the opening minutes, the Springboks could well have been further in arrears shortly afterwards when Poulton-Palmer turned on an even more spectacular run, which was talked about for years afterwards and which only just failed to take its place on the short list of Twickenham's greatest individual tries along with those of Obolensky and Hancock.

From a scrum a dozen yards inside the England half near the right touchline the ball came along the backs to Poulton-Palmer, who by rights should have continued the move towards the left corner flag. Instead he cut in and had the defence completely mixed up as he weaved through them and was through in the clear as he headed for what would have been a sensational 60-yard dash over to the right-hand corner. It seemed he had nothing to do but cross over for his second try when 'Boetie' McHardy appeared from nowhere, having dashed across from the other wing to bring him down right on the line.

A couple of weeks before this International, London Counties had been the third team (with Newport and Swansea) to beat these Springboks. Besides Poulton-Palmer, three others of those successful Londoners were in the England side this day (Poulton-Palmer's co-centre F. M. Stoop, fly-half W. J. A. 'Dave' Davies and 'Cherry' Pillman, the loose forward) and for the first twenty-five minutes of the match it seemed that they were inspiring their team mates to repeat the earlier triumph. England appeared to have complete command of the game. But in that twenty-fifth minute, the Springbok fly-half, Fred Luyt, made an opening and sent winger Jan Stegmann away. He had Jack Morkel in support and transferred to him as he came up to England full-back Johnston, for the Springbok centre to score the equalising try.

Against the run of the play, this was a turning point. The much bigger South African pack began to assert itself, and through into the second half, with the wind against them as well as having to contend with that great South African asset – forward strength – the England backs could not reproduce the winning sort of rugby they had displayed at the outset.

One of the batch of four Morkels, all related, in the Springbok side was D. F. T. (Duggie) Morkel, one of the most prodigious place-kickers the game has ever known. On their previous tour in 1906 it was he who had written into the record books rugby's longest measured shot at goal. The match was against Middlesex at Richmond and the county was penalised just inside the Springbok half. In those days penalty shots could be charged like kicks from a mark, so Morkel retreated a dozen yards to frustrate the charge before digging his hole. The kick was not successful but as it passed the posts it was almost at the height of the top of them and later when the measuring tape was brought out it was found that the distance from where he had kicked to where the ball pitched was 100 yards.

So in the second half when he was handed the ball for one long-range penalty and then another the hearts of the England supporters dropped each time. He confirmed their fears and South Africa emerged winners of the match 9–3.

That sadly put an end to England's unbeaten record at Twickenham, after three seasons at their new ground. But it continued to be a really lucky ground for England as far as their opponents in the Five Nations Championship were concerned. Not only were none of them able to record a win there from its opening until World War I but this state of affairs continued when International matches were resumed in 1920. It was not until 1926 that one of them, Scotland, managed to pull it off, which meant that (deducting the war years) for the first eleven seasons with Twickenham as their home ground England never lost

The International Situation 31

a Championship match there. In that period, only those two overseas giants, the Springboks (in 1913) and the All Blacks (in 1925) had lowered the England colours.

In fact, of their Championship rivals the Scots were the first to walk off the Twickenham turf as victors in 1926. Ireland had their first win there in 1929. The Welsh went until 1933 before they managed it. And France's great moment only came in 1951.

Chapter 4

The Wakefield Era

England have done the Grand Slam more than any of the others in the five nations of the championship – seven times, followed by Wales's six and one each for Scotland, Ireland and France – and no fewer than five of them came in that golden era just prior to and immediately following World War I. All too aware of England's in-and-out performance in the championship in the postwar years, one can only look back with envy at the excitement of being an England supporter in those days.

Just look at the record:

	1913			1921	
v. Wales	W	12–0	v. Wales	W	18–3
Ireland	W	15–4	Ireland	W	15–0
Scotland	W	3–0	Scotland	W	18–0
France	W	20–0	France	W	10–6

	1914			1922	
v. Wales	W	10–9	v. Wales	L	6–28
Ireland	W	17–12	Ireland	W	13–3
Scotland	W	16–15	Scotland	W	11–5
France	W	39–13	France	D	11–11

	1920			1923	
v. Wales	L	5–19	v. Wales	W	7–3
Ireland	W	14–11	Ireland	W	23–5
Scotland	W	13–4	Scotland	W	8–6
France	W	8–3	France	W	12–3

	1924	
v. Wales	W	17–9
Ireland	W	14–3
Scotland	W	19–0
France	W	19–7

The Wakefield Era

In a magnificent sequence of seven seasons (interrupted by the war) England played twenty-eight matches and lost only two of them, a run the like of which none of the other countries has ever approached. And the interesting thing about those two isolated defeats was that both of them were away, so that it was a glorious period for Twickenham fans.

The guiding genius who had got things started, Adrian Stoop, paved the way for the brilliant back play which was the dominant force behind England's two grand slams in the years before the Great War. The Royal Navy pair W. J. A. (Dave) Davies and F. E. Oakley were behind the scrum, Ronnie Poulton-Palmer at centre, with V. H. M. Coates and 'Kid' Lowe on the wings.

Lieutenant Oakley RN was lost at sea in one of HM submarines in the first months of the war. Poulton-Palmer, as we know, died on the Belgian Front in 1915. Coates, of whom O. L. Owen of *The Times* wrote 'a more formidable meteor never shot through the rugby sky', gave up the game after the war to concentrate on his medical practice. But Lowe was still in his prime when rugby resumed and in fact got the bulk of his record twenty-five consecutive caps in the years after that war. Scrum-half Dave Davies was also very much available, and he was to be joined by another RN colleague to form a pair that was to become more famous than the original Davies–Oakley combination – Davies and Kershaw.

So despite the unhappy loss of pre-war stars among the backs, England were still strong in that department. But if it had been brilliant back play that had been the basis of the success before the war, it was a superb pack that took England through their Championship triumphs of 1920 (shared), 1921, 1923 and 1924 – the Wakefield Era.

The name of Wakefield is indelibly linked with Twickenham. Born William Wavell Wakefield in 1898, he was educated at Sedbergh and Pembroke College, Cambridge, was a member of Parliament, Parliamentary Private Secretary to numerous Ministers, knighted in 1944 and created 1st Baron Wakefield of Kendal in 1963. A member of the RFU Committee and on the International Rugby Board, he was the Rugby Union's forty-second President in 1950–1. Among his friends and to the rugby public in general he was always known as 'Wakers' from that period of the 1920s when it was the vogue to use such terms as Twickers, champers, starkers and preggers. He held the record of most appearances for England for forty-two years. He is ranked as the greatest forward England has ever produced.

Wakefield went to war with the Royal Navy Air Service when he was eighteen and then transferred to the RAF, with whom he stayed

The men of the Wakefield Era of the early 1920s, the most successful period of England's rugby history: (standing) Hillard, Tucker, Hamilton-Wickes, Kittermaster, Gibbs, Davies, Young, Brough; (sitting) Cove-Smith, Blakiston, Voyce, Wakefield, Corbett, Conway, Edwards.

until 1923. It is not generally known what an all-round athlete he was. He was 440-yards champion for the RAF, he played cricket for the MCC, he was a Kandahar Gold skier, a water skier and a sub aqua diver.

He was captain of Cambridge at rugby in 1921–2 but he had received his England cap in 1920 in their first postwar International, in which their supporters confidently expected them to carry on their winning ways of pre-war seasons. But they were to be sadly disappointed, if only, as it turned out, momentarily.

For that opening International against Wales in 1920 the selectors had to rely to a certain extent on guesswork as to players' form after the disruption of the war. The 21-year-old Wakefield found himself in that match among a set of forwards whose names are not now remembered. At Swansea the England side were soundly beaten 19–5 in what came to be known as Jerry Shea's match. The Newport fly-half, who oddly enough was to be capped only twice again for Wales, scored 16 out of Wales's 19 points that day with a try, two dropped goals, a penalty and a conversion.

But after this setback new names were to appear among the forwards, men of the future who with Wakefield were to form the nucleus of the pack that was to bring England's golden era to its highpoint: G. S. Conway, of Cambridge, master of the now all but forgotten art of dribbling, inventor of the then sensational new technique of 'shin dribbling', a master at Rugby School and organiser of the RFU's Centenary Match there in 1923; R. Cove-Smith, another product of Cambridge, who was to captain the British Lions side in South Africa in 1924, a tour for which Wakefield was not available; W. G. E. Luddington, then an RN petty officer who had survived the war but was to be killed in action in World War II, a useful place-kicker as well as being a powerful front-row forward whose last minute conversion in the Calcutta Cup Match saved England's Grand Slam in 1923; A. F. Blakiston, of Northampton, who missed his Blue at Cambridge, the line-out specialist who in the loose was said to 'play his rugby like some Elizabethan adventurer, reckless, without ruth or fear'; Tommy Voyce, of Gloucester, with effective sight in only one eye following a war injury, an abrasive forward, often accused of being a leaner at scrum time, who became President of the RFU in 1960–1.

The contribution of Harlequins to the shape of English rugby is exemplified by the fact that Stoop had evolved the type of back play which made England dominant pre-war, while in the 1920s it was Wakefield, as a Harlequins regular, who developed what became known as 'back-row forward offensive and defensive tactics', which were the key to her continued success.

Today we take for granted the roles of the fast-breaking flankers and the No. 8 – quick to go into spoiling action when possession is lost at a scrum, linking with their own inside backs when the ball comes out the right way. But it was a novelty then, as executed by Wakefield, Blakiston and Voyce – a joy for England's supporters to watch and something which their opponents were quite unable to contend with. When the English pack got into its stride after that setback in the first International after the war, only once in five seasons were England thoroughly mastered and that was in the mud of Cardiff in 1922, when Wales emerged victors 28–6 after England had mistakenly persisted with the quick-moving tactics of their forwards in the loose when in the conditions keeping it tight was the only answer.

That, coupled with an 11–11 draw with Ireland, had cost England the Championship that year but 1923 and 1924 were both grand slam years again, and England were undoubtedly cock of the walk in rugby in Europe when New Zealand made the first of their postwar tours.

Chapter 5

The Brownlie Incident

There have been three 'incidents' at Twickenham – the sending-off of Cyril Brownlie during the England *v.* New Zealand match in 1925, which was sad, the presence of the 1969–70 Springboks accompanied by hordes of demonstrators and police, which was depressing, and a streaker's completely naked cross-field dash during the England–France charity match in 1974, which was hilarious.

ENGLAND *v.* NEW ZEALAND
3 January 1925

The teams:

England: J. W. Brough (Silloth); R. H. Hamilton-Wickes (Harlequins), V. G. Davies (Harlequins), L. J. Corbett (Bristol), J. C. Gibbs (Harlequins); H. J. Kittermaster (Oxford), A. T. Young (Cambridge); A. T. Voyce (Gloucester), A. F. Blakiston (Liverpool), G. S. Conway (Rugby), W. W. Wakefield (Harlequins, capt.), R. Cove-Smith (OMTs), R. J. Hillard (Oxford), J. S. Tucker (Bristol), R. Edwards (Newport).

New Zealand: G. Nepia; J. Steel, A. E. Cooke, J. S. Svenson; N. P. McGregor, M. F. Nicholls; J. J. Mill; J. H. Parker, J. Richardson (capt.), A. White, M. J. Brownlie, R. R. Masters, C. J. Brownlie, W. R. Irvine, Q. Donald.
Referee: A. E. Freethy (Wales).

So great was the public interest in this International, the first of the 1924–5 season, that not only was there a massive increase over the new Twickenham record of 43,000 spectators established in the last International of the previous season against Scotland; the 60,000 who crammed themselves into the ground represented the greatest number of people who had ever watched a rugby match in the game's history.

The magnet, of course, was that these All Blacks had won every match on their tour so far and this was their final game. Could England pull off what no other team in the British Isles had managed to achieve? As well as a contingent from Wales, who dearly hoped that England would emulate Wales putting paid to the 1905 All Blacks' unbeaten record, a large party of English people resident in Paris had braved gales in the Channel to see the match. Hordes of Scottish rugby fans, denied any sight of this great team because of Scotland's current involvement in a rugby political argument, poured out of their special

Crowd starts to build up for England *v.* New Zealand, 3 January 1925, to reach a then new record of 60,000.

trains at Euston to flock to Twickenham.

Not being an all-ticket match – a system which was not started at Twickenham until England's match with Wales in 1953 – the first arrivals at the ground were bright and early. In the words of *The Times*: 'Half a dozen enthusiasts, including girls, arrived outside Twickenham in the small hours of the morning and waited for patience to achieve what Joshua's trumpets are said to have accomplished more drastically in Biblical days.' (Ah, they don't write match reports like that any more.) By ten o'clock there were 5,000 people queued up outside to

be first in the rush to the unreserved accommodation, just recently enlarged by the addition of ringside seats and more spacious north and south terracing.

This period being what was to become known as the Dawn of the Motor Age, the rugby fans converged on Twickenham by car as never before. To guide them, plans had been published in the London papers showing the new 'motor parks' at the west and east sides of the ground and indicating all the 'motor entrances' through which they could be reached, the Wolseley company being smart enough to place an advertisement next to the maps extolling their 11/22 h.p. open tourer, £225 for the two-seater, the four-seater £10 extra. Just the thing for tootling off to Twickers clad in your 'Tweed Sports Suit of Jacket and "Plus Four" Knickers, price 59s 6d' advertised by the Army & Navy Co-operative Society Ltd.

Today motorists Twickenham-bound are aggravated by holdups on the broad Chertsey Road, the main artery from inner London, but it is as nothing compared to 1925 when motor cars, proliferating like rabbits in a warm mating season, made their way along what was then a narrow country road. Such was the congestion that it built up to an immovable traffic jam approaching the ground and it was only thanks to ex-King Manuel of Portugal that hundreds of ticket-holders were spared the disappointment of not getting to the ground for the kick-off. He lived on a large estate in that area and when police knocked on his door and asked whether they could divert the traffic across the fields in front of his manor he said by all means.

An hour before the two-thirty start all the unreserved space was filled and the gates were closed. Those who read their *Times* while waiting for the kick-off could not have regarded as a good omen the news of the other English sportsmen concurrently involved in an international match – England v. Australia in the Second Test in Melbourne. 'Australia's Record Score' said the headline and *The Times*, as was its wont in those days, went on to describe how the bowling of Mr J. W. H. T. Douglas and Mr A. E. R. Gilligan, assisted by the curtly named Tate and Woolley, had been hit all over the place in a most ungentlemanly manner by Mr Ponsford (128), Mr Richardson (138) and team mates to the tune of 600 runs.

Guests of honour at Twickenham were the Prince of Wales and the Prime Minister, Stanley Baldwin. When he went out on to the field to be introduced to the members of the two teams the bowler-hatted Prince carried a furled umbrella, mindful of all the rain there had been over the previous couple of days. But the weather stayed clear as the match blazed into action.

Blazed into action is no exaggeration. The two sets of forwards went

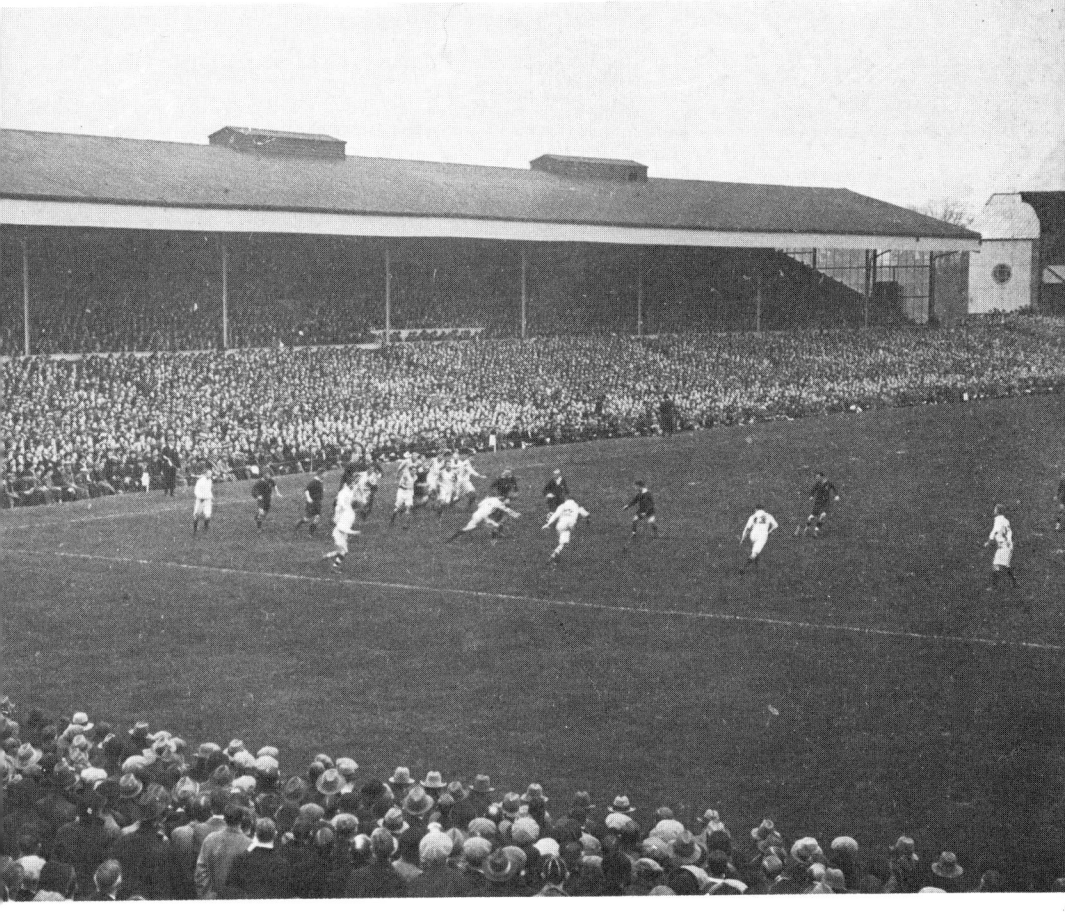

The All Blacks on the attack in England's encounter with New Zealand in 1925, when Cyril Brownlie was sent off.

at each other with such ferocity that more than once the referee, Alfred Freethy, had to stop play to issue warnings. Eventually, in the eighth minute, he ordered the All Black second-row forward Cyril Brownlie off the field.

In the welter of discussion, argument and confused recollection of the incident in the half-century that has followed the English tendency has naturally been to soft-pedal the whole affair and the New Zealand attitude has been to try to prove that an injustice was done.

In *The Times* report on the Monday the incident was dismissed with: 'There had been more than one unpleasant proof that the forwards were taking things too seriously and if Brownlie paid the penalty for ignoring the referee's warnings to both sides he had only himself to blame.'

In O. L. Owen's admirable *History of the Rugby Football Union*, published in 1955 and so thorough in all other respects, the only mention he makes of the matter is: 'The incidents which led to the sending off of Cyril Brownlie can now fairly be disregarded, even confined to the limbo of well-forgotten things.'

By contrast, *New Zealand Truth*, in their report from their correspondent at Twickenham, said after the match: 'There is little doubt that Mr Freethy made a mistake in dealing so drastically with Brownlie and there is every reason to suppose that he was considerably overwrought and excited with the fiery aspect of the opening play.'

In his Centennial Book of New Zealand Rugby, *On the Ball* (published in 1970), Gordon Slatter wrote:

> 'There were several different versions given of the incident that caused Brownlie to be ordered from the field only eight minutes after play had begun. One English player said this extreme punishment was meted out for backchat to the referee after being cautioned, another English player rather illogically stated that the referee had put his finger on the source of the trouble because after Brownlie's departure there was not a single untoward incident. One report said that it was for kicking a player on the ground, another said that the incident followed a scrummage in which A. T. Voyce of Gloucester was hurt in the mouth. Yet another account said the incident occurred in some loose play following a line-out. The New Zealanders were indignant that Brownlie should have been singled out because of his act of retaliation against a player who had been previously warned. They were even more indignant when they learned that this same player had been reported to the Rugby Football Union. They felt that if Cyril Brownlie had to be sent from the field, then Edwards of the bald head should have gone, too. It was no consolation that Edwards never again played for England. The New Zealand manager, Mr S. S. Dean, said that in the opinion of the All Blacks the referee had made a mistake.'

Apart from the white-wash aspects of Slatter's comments, his confusion as to what had actually happened reflects the many and varied versions of the activity leading up to the sending-off which have been voiced by all sorts of people over the years, including All Black participants in the match such as Mark Nicholls and George Nepia.

What nobody yet, to my knowledge, has seen fit to reprint is the account of the incident given by the person one would have thought was in the best position to know what happened – the referee. Either because the English, out of deference to the embarrassment the incident has caused to New Zealanders, have preferred to drop the matter, or because New Zealanders for their part find Alfred Freethy's statement explicitly damning, it has never been brought up.

On the Sunday after the match, in order to clear the air, the Rugby Football Union asked Mr Freethy to make a written statement and this was published in the morning papers of the Monday. It read: 'In some loose play the ball had been sent away and two or three England forwards were lying on the ground. C. Brownlie was a few feet away from them, and as he came back, he deliberately kicked on the leg an England forward lying face downward on the ground. I had taken my eye off the ball for a moment and therefore saw exactly what happened. Previous to this I had warned each side generally three times and therefore had no option but to send Brownlie off the field. I much regretted having to do this but in the circumstances I had no alternative but to take this drastic action.'

I was at Murrayfield when Colin Meads of the 1967 All Blacks became only the second of three ever to be sent off in an International, so I understand perfectly the feeling *The Times* correspondent was trying to get across in his report of the 1925 match when he wrote: 'In the hush of pained silence that followed the sending off of Brownlie, the game resumed . . .'

England went into attack and for a time had the advantage of playing against a disrupted New Zealand pack. In the All Blacks' 25 they cleverly wheeled a scrum and Wakefield and Voyce went away with the ball at their feet in a dribbling ploy typical of rugby at that time and done by none better than the England back row of the early 1920s. The ball was steered past Nepia and went over the line wide out. As two New Zealanders fumbled at the touchdown, Cove-Smith dashed in to throw himself on the ball. England 3, New Zealand 0.

New Zealand always packed 2–3–2 in those days, with a roving forward, a set-up which England rugbymen could never quite get the hang of, to the extent of the rover in this match, J. H. Parker, being listed in the programme alongside J. J. Mill as a half-back. When Brownlie had been sent off the New Zealand captain, Jock Richardson, had moved up from the back row to take his position and Parker packed in the scrum, with Mill taking on the unaccustomed task for a New Zealand half-back of putting the ball in.

When they settled down to this arrangement the All Black machine began rolling as effectively as it had done through the tour. There were no further incidents. The New Zealanders appeared to adjust better to what had then been an unprecedented occurrence; the English players seemed self-conscious about it.

After Nepia had found touch on the left near the England line there was some indecisive scrummaging, from which Maurice Brownlie got possession and went right. When he was checked the five-eighths executed a good change of direction and a long pass was shot out to Svenson on the left wing, for him to outpace the defenders for New Zealand's first try.

Their second, over on the other wing, was controversial. The All Blacks worked the blind side and the ball went out to Jack Steel, the powerful, determined winger. Not many years after this Steel was to be run over and killed and when his team mate Mark Nicholls was told the news he said, 'Impossible. Nothing could stop Jack Steel.' This day he made a typical aggressive run, twice barging would-be tacklers out of the way and each time, it seemed, putting a foot in touch before lunging over the line. Mr Freethy, aware of the reaction of the spectators on that touchline, ran over to consult the linesman before awarding a try amid a renewed outburst of booing. The touch judge on that side of the field was a member of the New Zealand party and right there and then it could have been a strong argument for having what did not come until a long time afterwards – neutral touch judges for Internationals.

With a 6–3 lead, New Zealand went further ahead just before the interval when the England forward Hillard unwisely got in front of the ball right before his own posts and Nicholls kicked an easy penalty. Half-time: England 3, New Zealand 9.

Ten minutes after the restart Maurice Brownlie, still smouldering inwardly about the ordering off of his brother, got the ball just inside the England 25. There seemed no way through the batch of defenders between him and the line. Outside him Jim Parker was better placed and called for the ball. Brownlie ignored him, put his head down and bulldozed his way through the Englishmen, two of them vainly clutching him as he smashed over the line. Walking back, Brownlie clearly felt that he had made a symbolic gesture, for he said to Parker: 'Jim, I wouldn't have passed it out for £100.'

The Nicholls conversion from a difficult angle made it 14–3 and then, twenty minutes from the end, when Parker himself barged over taking tacklers with him a 17–3 deficit looked too much for England to do anything about. But that last quarter turned out to be all theirs.

They made a magnificent fight-back. J. C. Gibbs, the Harlequins captain, making his debut for England as a last-minute replacement on the left wing, amazed everybody with his speed along the touchline and with only Nepia to beat he kicked over his head, not reckoning with the fact that the Maori teenager was wily far beyond his years and expert with the elbow out of viewing range of the referee. Gibbs failed to get to the ball in time. A couple of minutes later he was off again, precisely repeating the manoeuvre but this time steering clear of Nepia in the race for the ball. It was pure luck for the New Zealanders that Mill managed to appear on the scene for the forcedown.

The All Blacks now definitely seemed rattled. Second five-eighth McGregor got offside thirty yards out in front of the posts and in a moment of what turned out to be inspiration Wakefield tossed the ball to the centre L. J. Corbett. Brough, the full-back, had got nothing between the uprights in his numerous shots at goal and it seemed like desperation tactics on the part of Wakefield, since Corbett had no reputation whatsoever as a place-kicker. Surprised at being given the penalty, he made as if to punt to touch and then changed his mind. He signalled the touch judges around to the posts and then proceeded to put over a superb drop kick, which he confessed afterwards amazed and pleased him as much as it did the wildly cheering England supporters. England 6, New Zealand 17.

When they kicked off again after this the All Blacks worked their way to near the England line and then came by far the best of the match's six tries. When England got possession from a scrum their defending backs instead of kicking set off upfield and it went along the line to Hamilton-Wickes. He got through and started weaving in an effort to deceive Nepia, waiting for him just inside the New Zealand half. Nepia was not to be taken in. He stood his ground and just as it looked as though a great effort by the Cambridge right wing would be halted, the fly-half Kittermaster suddenly popped up inside him. He gave him a well-judged pass and Kittermaster ran fifty yards to score under the posts, the defence so split that nobody gave chase, the only time such a thing had occurred during the All Blacks' entire tour. This magnificent try was accorded what a contemporary report described as 'the greatest cheering ever known at Twickenham'. Conway converted and it was England 11, New Zealand 17.

However, the England rally had come too late. There were only a couple of minutes left for play and that proved to be the final score in a match which had started on a very unhappy note and then developed into a game thoroughly worthy of the record crowd it had attracted.

Chapter 6

The Twickenham Look

It was around this time between the wars that Twickenham began to take on the silhouette by which we recognise it today.

In the 1923-4 season more ringside benches had been added to those originally installed in 1921 and additions to the north and south terracing made room for a new record crowd of 43,000 to watch Wakefield's men score a splendid 19-0 victory in the Calcutta Cup match.

In 1925 the North Stand, with seats for 3,582, arose as it were on stilts above the terrace, and the West and East enclosures were augmented – all in time for a new record 60,000 to see that clash between England and the invincible All Blacks. With the building of this new stand spectators facing north were given a clock to watch as those famous 'dying minutes' of a match came up, rather than having to wrick their necks turning around to check the clock tower which used to stand behind the South Terrace, now replaced by the specially designed RFU weather vane.

In 1927, by a brilliant piece of architectural legerdemain, the East Stand got its upper deck without any disturbance of the original stand underneath, so that the whole is in effect – although one does not easily notice it – two grandstands sitting one upon the other, holding in all 12,000 people.

On 5 October 1929 the rather mean look of the main approach to the ground was given a more worthy appearance by the unveiling of the Rowland Hill Memorial Gates, as a mark of respect to the man who had died the previous year, after forty-nine years of service to the game.

In 1932, the Rugby Union having decided that more spacious committee rooms, offices, dressing-rooms etc. were needed, an entirely new double-decked West Stand was built at a cost of £75,025, the greatest single expenditure ever made at Twickenham. Outwardly it was a twin of the East Stand and likewise held 12,000. This, coupled with an extension of the South Terrace to bring its accommodation

Summer 1915. Horses keep the grass down during the war. This was the original Twickenham look with another single-decker (now the West Stand) out of view on the left.

to 20,000, paved the way for the pre-war record crowd of 73,000 to assemble in 1936 to see Prince Obolensky score one of Twickenham's most famous tries in England's 13-0 victory over the third All Blacks.

Along with all this construction the Rugby Union were mindful of the needs of the motorist. They had no choice but to be so, since from the end of the Great War to 1932 the number of cars on the road took a staggering jump from 77,707 to 1,127,681. The acquisition of seven acres for the West Car Park in 1923 proved quite inadequate to cope with the ever increasing number of those who wanted to go to

Twickenham by car. In 1925 the delightfully rural look of an orchard and an attractive old house called 'The Laurels' behind the East Stand was slashed asunder and the bare patch that was left became the East Car Park. But still this was not enough and a larger area was taken in to form the North Car Park in 1930, bringing the total parking space to 3,000 vehicles.

In 1932 the Rugby Union could have added to its now thirty acres when a further twenty-eight to the east of the ground came on the market. As well as additional parking space, this could have provided

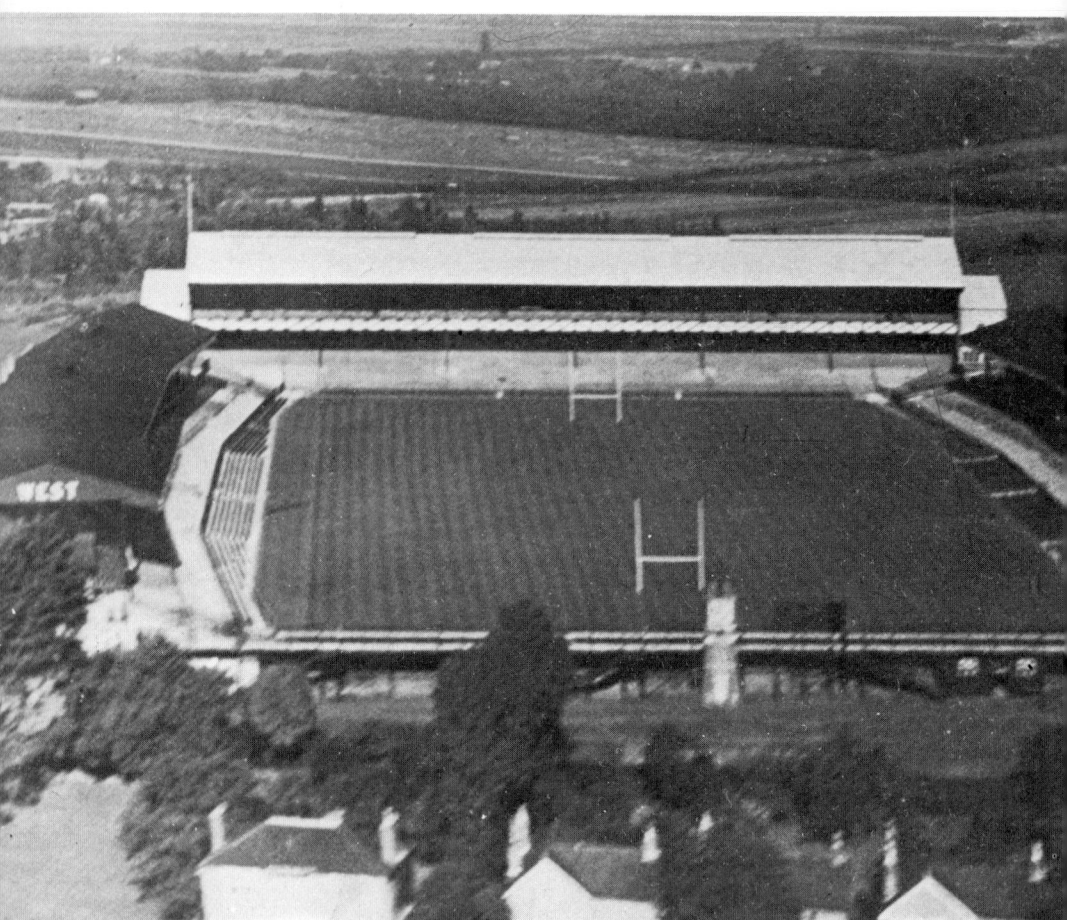

Twickenham 1925, on completion of the new North Stand. Clock tower and scoreboard are behind the South Terrace (foreground), to be replaced in 1950 by present weather vane.

a practice ground, which besides pleasing the players would have been heartily welcomed by the groundsman, who has never been happy about seeing his beloved turf churned up during England training sessions. But the RFU committee of that period thought twice about it and were then too late to make the purchase. In the dozen or so years since the end of the Great War they had spent over £150,000 on Twickenham (a considerable sum in those days) and were heavily into the bank. And that year of 1932 was hardly the one in which to think of expansion. It was then that the Depression reached its nadir and the most used word in the business section of the newspapers was 'retrenchment'.

So it was that the physical appearance of Twickenham as we know it now was settled in the early 1930s. Almost as soon as the Depression was over we became involved in World War II and, after the war, the Rugby Union had too much on its hands merely getting the ground back into shape to have time to start about further building and improvement.

There was, however, an addition to the Twickenham skyline in 1950, when the weather vane (used as an attractive background to the opening of many a television broadcast from the ground) rose above the South Terrace at the spot the old clock tower used to occupy. It is as familiar to sports enthusiasts now as its cousin, the Father Time weather vane at Lord's. Pleasingly designed by Kenneth Dalgleish it depicts the winged messenger, Hermes, life-size (if that can be said of one of the immortal gods), sending out a well-directed pass to a modern rugby player heading for the posts, with the RFU insignia underneath.

In that same year of 1950, Twickenham achieved its all-time record crowd of 75,157 for the England–Wales game. The ground could then rightfully be said to be one with a 75,000 capacity but neither the Rugby Union nor the police had been entirely happy about that record gathering and on the basis of comfort and security it was decided that henceforth there would be a restriction to 72,500.

By the 1960s the Rugby Union felt that the time was appropriate to launch into further development of the property. Plans were drawn up to rebuild the South Terrace with an upper deck that would be more spacious than its counterpart to the north. The new project would provide room for a further 8,000 people, to boost Twickenham's capacity to over 80,000 and make it the biggest rugby ground in Britain, outdistancing Murrayfield, which holds the Home Countries' official record with 78,500 for the Calcutta Cup match of 1962 and an undisclosed figure in excess of that for the overcrowded Scotland–Wales match in 1975.

Brilliant piece of engineering in 1927 saw top deck of East Stand being erected without disturbing accommodation of original single-decker – in effect one stand sitting on top of another.

However, there were snags. The chief groundsman, Harold Clark, had worries about a drying problem on the pitch if the proposed 90-foot high structure went up at that end of the ground. Even as things were it has always been necessary to open up broad panels at the back of the northern terrace, when spectators are not around, so that any wind that is about can feel free to drive across the turf and aid in dehydrating it. But after much consultation about prevailing winds and other considerations these fears were allayed.

Then there was the matter of ancient lights, what are legally 'the rights of light enjoyed by a property owner over adjoining land, no building being permissible that would seriously interfere with that privilege'. Although they do now, the Rugby Union did not at that time own all the houses along the rear of the South Terrace and there could be objections to what amounted to a skyscraper going up outside the back windows of a householder. Before planning permission could be obtained a public enquiry had to be held.

The Rugby Union emerged from that successfully but the period of discussion and negotiation extended not merely over months but years and by then another snag arose. The original costings on the project had meanwhile skyrocketed and at length it was felt that far too much money would be involved. Reluctantly the whole thing had to be shelved.

So, apart from various additions and improvements that have been made at Twickenham in recent years, this is how the ground organisation remains:

Covered Seating

Lower West Stand	6,500
Upper West	5,500
Lower East	6,500
Upper East	5,500
Upper North	3,500
Total	27,500

Open Seating　　　　　　　　　　　　　　　*Standing*
Ringside 5,000　　　　　　　　　　　　　　Terraces 40,000

Grand total: 72,500

There has, however, been a radical alteration to the look of the ground. This latest – and most unexpected – change in the appearance of Twickenham came on 1 January 1973. One would have thought that the Rugby Football Union would have been one of the last strongholds against the invasion of the hard sell. But no. On that date advertisement boards were seen to adorn – oldtimers would undoubtedly have said desecrate – the perimeter and the balcony of the East Stand.

Although for many years a commonplace at soccer grounds and for a number of years in evidence at Lord's cricket ground, it might have been argued that it was all right in such places, since after all those are professional sports. But in 1972 Cardiff Arms Park and Murrayfield had succumbed, so that when advertisers put the pressure on the Committee of the RFU, the Committee yielded. The point

New East Stand comes into use at beginning of 1927–8 season. Old West Stand was pulled down and completely rebuilt as double-decker in 1931 after utility type entrance (right foreground) had been replaced by Rowland Hill Gates in 1929.

was, why turn down a handsome bit of extra annual revenue which could be put to the general benefit of the game?

Arena Sports, of Thornton Heath, handle the operation for the Rugby Union. They are the experts. They also cover Wembley, Hampden Park, and so on. The charge to advertise at Twickenham – at the time of writing – is £5,000 per season for a standard-sized panel and the cut the Rugby Union receives from all advertising fees is £40,000 a year.

Chapter 7

That Immaculate Turf

One of the things that makes the greatest impression on anyone visiting Twickenham for the first time is of course that glorious strip of immaculate turf.

Wembley and Cardiff Arms Park (since the Welsh Rugby Union got rid of its quagmire reputation by moving the Cardiff club off it to the pitch next door) have playing surfaces of which they are proud but what the general public does not realise is that, apart from important matches, those grounds are very little used. Twickenham, on the other hand, has to stand up to an average of thirty matches a year. Besides the showpieces (the Internationals, the Varsity Match and the Middlesex Sevens), Harlequins still have fixtures there despite the fact that they now have their own ground. There are the three Inter-Services matches, Schools Internationals, the Club Knock-Out Final and the Final Trial, not to mention the England squad's training sessions on the pitch.

In spite of all that activity the field of play seems not to have a blade of grass out of place as the crowd waits for the teams to appear on International days. How is it done? That is the secret of Yorkshireman Harold Clark, Clerk of Works and Ground Superintendent.

He does not agree with that well-known anecdote about an American tourist looking over an English estate saying to the head gardener, 'Tell me, how do you get such beautiful lawns?' and being told, 'It's simple. All you need to do is mow them and roll them for 300 years.'

The Twickenham turf is never rolled. 'The place for a roller', says Clark, 'is in the shed going rusty.'

Rolling, he will tell you, merely adds to that menace of 'compaction', of which even those of us who merely have a strip of lawn in the back garden know something, as witness the spiking we do in spring to give the roots of the grass a chance to spread and to prevent surface water from collecting. At Twickenham there is a fearsome-looking array of mechanical spikers and as an additional method of combating compaction Clark some years ago helped to invent a system called 'sand slitting' which is now used all over the world by groundsmen at sports arenas and anywhere else where big stretches of grass have to be kept in good condition. This consists of making slits in the ground fifteen inches deep and a foot apart and dumping tons of sand into them, and today a big industry has built up for manufacturing sand slitting machines that can be driven back and forth across a field covering the whole job in one operation.

Every four years the entire Twickenham pitch is ploughed up. 'It looks a hell of a mess', says Clark. This, it seems hardly necessary to mention, is done in the off season, in May, and the ground is sown with half a ton of seed (nothing but rye grass because that is what stands up best to wear and tear). Within seven weeks it looks like a lawn again and by the opening of the season in September nobody could tell that it had been ravaged.

Seeding goes on all through the winter on any places that start to look bare. Returfing is never done. Clark will admit that they do from time to time move a bit that has not had much wear, from behind the goal posts, say, to somewhere that has been getting a little too much scrummaging but new turf is never brought in for patching up. This goes right along with the tradition at Twickenham that everything must look neat and tidy. 'Grass comes in many different shades of green', says Clark. 'You just can't match them and it would be awful for spectators to look down at the pitch and see a bit of patching that didn't fit in with the rest.'

Mainly as a protection against frost, the grass is kept three to four inches high, which means that when you are standing on it you are literally ankle deep. England players are accustomed to this, as are the regulars in the other teams in the International Championship, but newcomers in the touring All Blacks, Wallabies or Springboks find it disconcerting.

I remember asking the fleet-footed New Zealand wing, Ron Jarden, on his first visit to England what he thought of the Twickenham turf and he echoed the feelings of many of his colleagues from abroad that 'it's like running around on a spring mattress'. To New Zealanders, and more especially to South Africans accustomed to their sparsely grassed pitches, the contrast underfoot takes a time to get used to. They know that the Rugby Union likes to have the field looking immaculate for an International but they have been heard to mutter that there is a hint of gamesmanship in the fact that touring teams can do no training beforehand on the sacred turf and the first feel they get of it is when they trot out for their first match at Twickenham.

From the first International in 1910 right through to the present only

Some twenty tons of straw are needed when frost threatens Twickenham. Viewing the situation here are Sir William Ramsay, Honorary Treasurer for twenty years, Robin Prescott, Secretary 1963–73, C. H. Gadney, distinguished referee and President 1962–3, and A. R. F. Wright, now archivist to the RFU.

one big game at Twickenham has ever been postponed because of the weather – the England–France match of 1947.

The big menace of course is the ground being frozen. At Murrayfield, that problem was solved when a local rugby enthusiast made them a present of an underground heating system. At Twickenham, as any English fan knows, it is all done with straw and Clark and his staff have to be constantly on the qui vive about any sudden drop in temperature that is likely to necessitate their getting to work with the pitchforks.

Naturally they are in close touch with the Weather Centre, which is the term everybody uses now instead of the Meteorological Office because nobody could ever get their tongue around it properly.

And it would seem that at the Centre they are just as keen as rugby followers not to be caught napping at Twickenham and get stuck with a frozen ground. As far as the weathermen are concerned it is a case of 'don't call us we'll call you'. Clark never has to phone them. They always take it upon themselves to get in touch with him about the state of the weather when the time is coming up to a big match.

Oddly enough, as well as this expert advice, something else which Clark relies upon for advance warning of cold weather moving in are the aeroplanes which fly over the ground.

Anybody who has been to Twickenham cannot help but be aware, when the big planes zoom across over the stands, that the ground is on one of the main routes to and from Heathrow Airport, just a few miles to the west. Planes, of course, take off and land against the wind. So, when you see a jumbo jet flying over the ground towards the west you know that it is coming in to land, flying against the wind from the west, and if it is flying to the east it has taken off against the wind from that quarter. And when it is the latter case – that is bad news for the ground staff, since in the winter it is the east wind that brings in the cold weather. Clark is a busy man and cannot be expected to be watching planes all the time, so from the kitchen window of their cottage across the way from his office under the North Stand his wife keeps a lookout and when the worst happens she runs across to tell him, 'The planes are flying to the east!', and the ground staff go on Straw Alert.

Incidentally, talking of planes over Twickenham, when pilots know that they have a batch of rugbymen on board, they always drop a wing over Twickenham so that they can get a good view of the ground. A friend of mine who flew out from Heathrow with a group of supporters to see some of the 1974 Lions matches in South Africa told me that their pilot afforded them a splendid passing vista of Twickenham. 'It looked so *big*', he said, and then he added, 'Of course there had to be some bloke at the back of the plane who shouted "Come on, Wales!"'

For anti-frost cover, a quantity of between fifteen and twenty tons of straw is used and anyone who has ever been confronted with the job of manhandling that amount of straw over an area of some 80 yards by 150 yards knows that it takes some shifting. The more helpers there are on hand the better.

I remember when the 1967 All Blacks were to play the South of Scotland at the Greenyards ground at Melrose there was danger of frost putting paid to the match, so the straw was brought on the day before. To get it all down, inmates from the nearby mental hospital were recruited and when they were waving their pitchforks around I was a bit wary of them, until assured that they were under sedation.

While I was watching one of them at work he said to me: 'The All Blacks are no' going to like this.'

'Why not?' I asked.

'It'll slow 'em up something terrible.'

At Twickenham the ground staff of twelve have time to spread the straw, having had plenty of advance notice thanks to the Weather Centre and Mrs Clark's plane spotting. But getting it all off for the match to take place, that is the tough part. They dare not remove it too soon in case the frost gets into the ground before kick-off. So, having devoted a couple of days to getting the field's straw covering on, they can only allow themselves three hours to take it all off. Therefore, anybody who happens to be around at the ground before the scheduled start is likely to find he has a pitchfork shoved into his hand and is told to get on with it. But just as cricket spectators at a rainy Test Match will volunteer to help the ground staff mop up so that play can get under way, nobody minds in the least lending a hand to clear the decks for action at Twickenham.

The ground's tall, gracious goalposts are not the highest of the world's International grounds. The 65 feet of those at Eden Park, Auckland, and the 60 feet at Ellis Park, Johannesburg, for example, are considerably taller than Twickenham's 45-footers, but without visits these days by such prodigious place-kickers as Don Clarke and Okey Geffin it is very rare at Twickenham for the touch-judges to be placed in doubt by a ball going over the top of the posts.

The posts are in fact ship's masts, diverted from their ocean-going function to do duty at the ground when the original ones were presented to Rugby School in 1956. They have a hollow core and are of laminated 15-inch wooden sections for strength. Each upright has a 4-foot zinc 'shoe', inserted into concrete blocks under the turf. The shoe is tapered, so that when the post is wedged into the slot in the concrete there is a bit of play at the bottom to compensate for swaying in the wind.

Over the years the ground staff have come to know that it takes an hour to put the posts up and an hour and a half to take them down and this bit of time-and-motion study proved invaluable during the 'demo tour' of the 1969–70 Springboks. Four matches were to be played at Twickenham. The RFU officials knew and the demonstrators knew that the simplest and most effective way of making a rugby ground unusable is to get rid of the goalposts. So to frustrate the demonstrators' schemes the ground staff had the chore of removing the crossbars and hiding them before each match, then putting them

A couple of Welshmen getting an upside down view of one of Don Rutherford's penalties in England's 14–6 win over Wales in 1960. Note lack of padding at the base of the 45 ft goal posts – not added until 1972.

up just before the game started and taking them down again right after it was finished.

Although it had long been customary in New Zealand, Australia and South Africa to pad the bottom of the goalposts as a safeguard against would-be try-scorers knocking themselves out cold in a misdirected dive for the line, this did not come to Twickenham until 1972. The padding is strange-looking spongey stuff of green flecked with brown, known in the trade as 'potato foam'. It is two and a half inches thick and is wrapped around the base of the uprights encased in a tailor-made plastic jacket, to form what they call at Twickenham 'gaiters'.

Another matter on which observers often remark is the tidiness of Twickenham. On match days there is no evidence whatsoever of all the paraphernalia one knows must be there for the care and maintenance of that stretch of turf and the stands and terraces surrounding it.

Underneath the North Terrace, securely locked behind sliding doors on the day of a match, there is a row of workshops and storerooms the complexity of which the majority of people who go to Twickenham never realise. There are vast stores of everything from timber and paint to grass seed and toilet paper. A huge collection of mowers, spikers, sanders, grass brushers and all the other things needed to manicure the turf – including the roller rusting from disuse. A joinery shop, where among other things new grandstand seats are made on the premises; a metal works and plumber's; a paintshop, with signwriting department, constantly busy keeping up with the souveniring of notices all round the ground (LADIES is the one that disappears most often). It is amazing the amount and variety of work the Clerk of Works and his staff of twelve get through; it has to be a construction job of major proportions before any outside firm is called in.

It is not until the Thursday after an International that Twickenham is immaculately tidy again, since it takes that long to clear up the mess we 70,000 visitors have made of it. And included in the clearing up operation is the assembling of lost property.

Single gloves top the list of items left behind, in keeping with the experience of railway and bus lost property offices in winter time, but not umbrellas, which is usual with trains and buses. Twickenham used to accumulate piles of lost umbrellas but now they are a rarity, which could either be a reflection of the fact that our winters are indeed becoming less unpleasant or it merely ties in with the fact the more casual gear worn by people these days does not require the same sort of rain protection.

A man's odd shoe is often to be found in the stands after a match and this somewhat baffles the Rugby Union. It does not surprise them that a man might take a shoe off to ease a corn, but they wonder how he got home. Women do it differently. They leave pairs of shoes, neatly side by side in the West Car Park. However, it did not take the Rugby Union long to figure that one out. Clearly what happens is that a woman coming out to her car after a match will change into her driving shoes, have her attention distracted by a post mortem about the game and drive off leaving her walking shoes there on the ground.

A great proportion of the items are claimed by phone within a couple of days of the big game but the staff at Twickenham are set some posers, as 'I think I lost an ear-ring in the West Stand, could you please find it?' (They did.) The most unusual bit of lost property was a man's pair of trousers and how *he* got home the Rugby Union have given up trying to figure out.

For the spectators at Twickenham there are 30 lavatories, 17 for the men and 13 'Ladies'. There are 186 toilets, the most for any sports ground in Britain.

When rugby started to enter the boom period it is now enjoying many soccer fans made the switch from their own game, but unfortunately when they came from such grounds as Highbury and White Hart Lane to Twickenham they brought some of their bad habits with them, not the least of which was the throwing of toilet rolls on to the pitch.

Not unnaturally this unheard-of desecration of the Twickenham turf horrified the powers-that-be. What was to be done about this unhappy development? A meeting was held and the then secretary, Robin Prescott, an incisive man, solved the problem in a twinkling. 'The answer is simple, gentlemen', he said. 'We just switch to Jeyes' squares.' Which they did and since then never again has a white streamer been seen to snake its way across the hallowed turf.

Chapter 8

The Great Varsity Match

It was between the wars that the Varsity Match came to Twickenham, but to put this subject into proper perspective it is necessary to jump forward in time to the 1970s.

On 10 December 1974 Twickenham received the best bit of news it had had for a long time. The occasion was the playing of the 93rd University Match and the reason the news was good was that the fixture, having gone into steady decline as to quality of play and attendance in the preceding years, abruptly, dramatically, came alive again.

At the resumption of the annual meeting between Oxford and Cambridge after the war, in 1946, there had been a then record attendance of 44,000 people. It was felt that even more would be attracted if the match were switched from the traditional Tuesday to a Saturday. This was tried in the following year. The result was that the crowd dropped to 38,000 and the experiment was not tried again. In 1949 the attendance rocketed to a new record of 59,400 and through the 1950s that was the sort of well-filled Twickenham one became accustomed to for the Varsity Match.

But the 1960s were not far advanced before something of a rot had set in. Successive disappointing matches, in which the standard of rugby appeared to be getting progressively worse, meant that the crowds dwindled and by the 1970s few over and above the ardent faithfuls attended. Attendance sank to below half what had become regarded as the usual crowd for the fixture in the postwar years. 'Coming to the Varsity Match this year?' . . . 'No, I don't think I'll bother' became a cliché of the rugby world.

But then, as the 1974–5 season got under way, the apathy became less marked. The main reason for this was that both Oxford and Cambridge, whose performances against major clubs in the warm-up period before the Varsity Match had for some years been undistinguished, suddenly started recording very worthwhile victories. Oxford easily disposed of Northampton, Cardiff and Gloucester.

Cambridge went even better by beating Richmond, London Scottish, Blackheath and Harlequins and drawing with Northampton. This did not go unnoticed by the general rugby public and in the weeks preceding the 10 December 1974 clash the talk got around that 'this could well be a much better Varsity Match'.

So strong was the hope that this time the fixture might regain something of its former stature, that the most unfavourable weather for rugby – bitterly cold wind with the hint of rain if not snow in the air – did not deter an extra 10,000 people over and above the sad postwar low of the previous year from making their way to Twickenham.

The two teams rose to the occasion. Before it was over we had seen a match not on the level, as of late with this fixture, of Clifton playing Cheltenham in a bad year but up to the standard of an International – and streets ahead of many that had been seen in recent years. Cambridge in particular turned on slick, well trained rugby (under their coach Ian Robertson). Quick possession from efficient rucking had little Richard Harding sending his backs away time and again on exciting moves. Oxford, with not so much possession, had a solid defence which prevented the Light Blues from running away with the game and their exciting forays came mainly from individual breaks when a Cambridge attack had been halted. The match was played at a cracking pace, despite referee Ken Pattinson's insistence on instantly penalising infringements instead of playing the advantage rule.

What was so rewarding about this Varsity Match and raised hopes that it was a turning point for university rugby was that the players were predominantly of the 'first Blue' category. The much talked-of Cambridge fly-half Alan Wordsworth, regarded as an England star to be, had to stand down through injury and his replacement, a twenty-year-old Scot, Nigel Breakey, acquitted himself admirably. There were only two Internationals on the field, the Cambridge centres Peter Warfield, with three England caps, and Mike O'Callaghan, with three appearances for New Zealand. The only other person to take the field with any sort of name as far as the general public was concerned was the Oxford left wing Raymond Burse, whose reputation, however, was strictly potential. An American coloured athlete, he was being played after merely one previous first-class rugby match but it was felt that he was possessed of such speed that he could set things alight for Oxford. His pre-match publicity undoubtedly helped to swell the crowd but to their disappointment those inside him for some odd reason felt it best to kick ahead rather than pass the ball to him so he was never really unleashed.

From the unknowns Alistair Hignell, the Cambridge full-back, was to single himself out as a definite England prospect in that position where a permanent replacement for Bob Hiller was needed. Besides performing well the duties expected of a full-back, including place-kicking, Hignell showed great flair in attack, especially when he made a break after he had joined the three-quarter line and sent Gordon Wood away on the wing, then to be on hand to take an inside pass and score.

This came half way through the second half to bring Cambridge's score to 16, Hicknell's contribution being this try, two penalties and conversion of a Warfield try following a powerful run-in from thirty yards. But while they were piling up these 16 points Oxford had been keeping in touch thanks to some great goal-kicking by their fly-half, Nigel Quinnen. Three of his successful penalties took the score to 16–9. Then just after Hicknell scored his try Quinnen made it 16–12 with another. Then two minutes later, to thunderous applause, he kicked Oxford to merely one point behind the Light Blues, 16–15.

Twickenham was in excited uproar with fifteen minutes to go and anybody's game. Both teams were going all out, with such things happening as Oxford's full-back Waterman opening up from behind his own goal line. Then, just a couple of minutes before full time there was complete silence as Quinnen tee-ed up a 45-yard penalty attempt. If he had landed his sixth penalty, to bring his side victory by 18 points to 16, he would have made himself an ever-remembered Oxford rugby hero. But it fell short and perhaps it was only fair that it did. On the run of play Cambridge had been clearly the better side, and to have scored two tries and been beaten by six penalties would have been an almost exact repeat of that notorious Don Clarke 18–16 victory over the 1959 Lions.

There was only one sour note in this best Varsity Match for many a year and that was the final whistle of Referee Pattinson, who further infuriated many of the onlookers by concluding proceedings in the thirty-ninth minute of the second half, when everybody was looking forward to at least three or four minutes of injury time of a game nobody wanted to end.

But no matter. As Barry John wrote the next day: 'The Varsity Match is back on the rugby map.'

The first University match was played in the Parks at Oxford on 10 February 1872, just a year after the first-ever International. It was on the initiative of H. A. Hamilton, later Canon Douglas-Hamilton, of Cambridge, and it was also his initial suggestion that the fixture be played at the neutral ground after Oxford had won that pioneer match at the Parks and Cambridge won the return game at home. The

Oval became the venue for the next clash in the first half of the 1873-4 season and it continued to be played at the cricket ground until 1879, when England also gave up the Oval as a setting for their Internationals. From 1880 to 1886 the Varsity Match was played at the Rectory Field, Blackheath, before a further switch took the fixture to a ground which was a great favourite with the oldtimers – the Queen's Club. There it remained for thirty-four years, interrupted only by the war, and then Twickenham became its new and permanent home in December 1921.

Playing the match on a Tuesday in December became a tradition and only that once in modern times, in 1947, has there been a deviation to what may have seemed to be a more logical Saturday. This was only partly because the organisers felt that an even bigger crowd would turn up; they were influenced by a Government appeal to sports bodies not to break into the working week if possible, at that time of economic crisis for Britain. In the event, the attendance slumped. Almost as soon as the Tuesday fixture was reinstated the record 59,400 was achieved in 1949.

It is as well that the match does fall on a Tuesday for, besides its distinctive social side as a great get-together of Oxbridge students present and past, it has that other characteristic of large patronage by parties of schoolboys shepherded by games masters (doling out pre-match Mars bars and other goodies bought in bulk), which one does not see to the same extent at Twickenham for Saturday fixtures.

From the earliest days of Internationals the influence of Oxbridge on the game was tremendous. The tactical side of that influence was represented in the 1910s and the 1920s by two Cambridge men, first Stoop and then Wakefield, who revolutionised England's ideas of back play and forward play.

In regard to contributing players to the British Lions touring sides, so important were the two universities at the outset that only in recent years have Cambridge and Oxford respectively been toppled from first and fourth places in the list of most Lions from any one club over the years.

When England played South Africa at Twickenham in 1913, six of the England side were Oxford or Cambridge men. For the match against New Zealand in 1925 there were no fewer than eight.

Such an important nursery for England players was the Varsity Match that it was regarded as an extra Trial, players being excused duty in the regular Trials to go on display before the selectors in the university clash at Twickenham. And not only were the English selectors interested. When England went north of the border on

25 March 1925 to play the Calcutta Cup match which marked the official opening of Murrayfield, six of their team were from Oxbridge, but Scotland outdid the visitors by fielding seven – a total of 13 Oxford and Cambridge men in the one International!

And so it went on. In England's match with Wales at Twickenham in 1935, a total of eleven Varsity Match products took the field, five for England and six for Wales.

Into the 1950s: seven Oxbridge men were in the England team that won in the last minute that notorious game against the 1958 Australians.

Right into the 1960s: in the England v. Ireland match at Twickenham in 1960, there were eight from the universities in the England team; for the match against France in 1963, eight again!

And what stars they were, those Varsity men, not just fly-by-night players who happened to scrape a cap for their country.

In the 1910s – Stoop, 'Kid' Lowe and Poulton-Palmer. In the 1920s – Wakefield, Blakiston, Conway, Cove-Smith, Kittermaster for England and the dominant force in Scottish rugby, the best three-quarter line that country has ever produced, A. C. Wallace, G. G. Aitken, G. P. S. Macpherson and I. S. Smith, direct from their Varsity Match triumphs for Oxford. In the 1930s – England stars Aarvold, Candler, Cranmer, Cannell, Obolensky and Owen-Smith and the Welsh notables Viv Jenkins and Wilf Wooller. In the 1950s – Jeeps, Horrocks-Taylor, Hetherington, Kendall-Carpenter, Marques and Currie, Peter Robbins and Chris Winn, with Andy Mulligan, of Ireland, Gordon Waddell, of Scotland, and Clem Thomas, of Wales, regular visitors to Twickenham. In the 1960s – Sharp, John Spencer, John Roberts, John Young, Phillips, Danny Hearn, Hiller and Harding, and the great Mike Gibson, of Ireland.

Where are the new Varsity stars of International stature today? In the England sides of the mid-1970s only the solitary Peter Dixon seemed to be carrying the flag on behalf of the two once great rugby universities.

The rot set in as the 1960s were drawing to a close and there appeared to be three basic reasons why the Varsity Match had dwindled in esteem and was in danger of no longer being a healthy breeding ground for International players of class. One was that with the burgeoning clamour for university places in Britain, those in control of the intake of students at Oxford and Cambridge were placing much more accent on the academic standards of the applicants. Aptitude at sport did not carry the same sort of weight as formerly in tipping the balance as to whether or not you got to Oxbridge. So, not only with rugby, but with cricket too, the quality suffered. Secondly, with rugby a booming sport more and more young men not of public school and varsity background were coming into the game and tending to dominate it. And thirdly, linked closely with that second reason, with coaching and training making rugby an altogether sterner game in Britain the varsity approach, although once so admirable, could not quite stand up to the new demands.

Thankfully, however, those people who were prepared to put the Varsity Match into the same category as the Eton and Harrow match at Lord's and other such traditional events which have declined, have been proved wrong. Or at least there is great hope that they have.

Chapter 9

The Booming Sevens

In contrast to the Varsity Match, another annual event which has never dwindled in interest, but has always been on a rising graph of popularity since it came to Twickenham in 1926, is the last fixture of the season – the Middlesex Sevens.

Some people are not enthusiastic about seven-a-side rugby. To them it is too much rich food, too much open play and none of the arts of full scrummaging and the line-out, too many 70-yard tries, an aspect of rugby which they feel should not be commonplace, as in sevens, but should be an isolated treasured memory as in the fifteen-man game. But the whole point of the Middlesex Sevens is that it is a fun day – Twickenham *en fête* before the close-down for the summer months.

Not for one moment does the Middlesex County RFU, who organise the picnic, claim to have invented the seven-a-side game.

If you ever happen to be in the charming townlet of Melrose, in the Scottish borders, you cannot help but notice the Greenyards rugby ground. After all, what has Melrose got but a high street, a boys' prep school, a nine-hole golf course in the shadow of the Eildons, a ruined abbey, a thriving mental hospital – and Greenyards, where they play rugby to the sound of the nearby River Tweed in winter spate. Across the road from the ground is a pub called the King's Arms, where in framed pictures on the walls is unfolded the history of sevens.

It seems that in 1882 the Melrose club fell into financial difficulties. (Interesting how money problems can give rise to traditional rugby fixtures – the Wallabies at the end of their 1948 tour of Britain had a cash shortage and the Barbarians came to their aid with a fund-raising match which is now the established last match of all major tours to the UK.) A member of Melrose, the local butcher, had the inspired idea of staging an inter-club tournament in which teams of seven-apiece would play a modified form of rugby. Little did he know that Sevens would at once catch on as a diverting variation of the game, being embraced far more quickly than the much publicised effort to get

Plus-fours of the 1930s very much in evidence in this 1932 picture of spectators allowed on to the field during the interval at the Middlesex Sevens to play 'thousand-a-side rugby'.

today's youngsters interested in a complicated ten-a-side version.

The end-of-the-season sporting and social aspect of Sevens made an instant appeal to players south of the border and English and Welsh clubs flocked north to take part in the annual tournaments which were to be organised not only by Melrose but also neighbouring border clubs Galashiels and Hawick. Inevitably sevens – like that other great Caledonian product, Scotch whisky – was deemed eminently exportable and it was brought south in 1926 by a Scotsman, Dr Jimmy Russell-Cargill, then a member of the Middlesex Committee and later

President – which explains why the trophy presented to the seven-a-side winners at the end of the day at Twickenham is called the Russell-Cargill Memorial Cup.

Fifty clubs entered for that first tournament in 1926 and it was won by Harlequins, captained and inspired by – of course – W. W. Wakefield. He led them to victory again in the following year. And the next. In 1929 when they won it for the fourth time running, with Wakefield in his thirty-second year, it seemed that Harlequins were the unassailable masters of the seven-a-side technique. But in 1930 London Welsh moved in and since then honours have been shared with such as Blackheath, Richmond, Rosslyn Park, Loughborough Colleges and London Scottish, the last two having a period during the 1960s when no club was able to stop one or the other from coming out on top.

An essential of the concept of the Middlesex Sevens was that it was for charity and the Middlesex Hospital Cancer Fund being designated it received a very useful cheque for £1,621 8s 7d from the first tournament. This had risen to well over £4,000 after the war but when the Labour Government nationalised the hospitals the Middlesex Committee were shocked to find that the annual Sevens donation was not going to their chosen charity but instead was being diverted elsewhere. So the financial arrangements were changed. A Middlesex County RFU Memorial Fund was set up, and now takings from the Sevens go to the making of loans to clubs to purchase grounds, erect pavilions and so on and to charitable purposes such as assisting physical education and the relief of distress. That original £1,600 has now risen to £38,000 from the 1975 finals.

The increase reflects the huge growth in the popularity of the event. The 50-club entry of the first tournament has now leapt up to 298 in 1975. Originally a self-contained competition at Twickenham, by 1950 so many clubs were clamouring to enter that the system had to be introduced of playing preliminary rounds on other grounds on the preceding Saturday – teams fighting it out on twenty pitches at eight grounds for most of the day to arrive at the twelve who would join the previous year's finalists and the two guest sides to make up the sixteen for the knock-out on finals day at headquarters.

Anyone going to the Sevens at Twickenham for the first time finds that although the attendance falls not far short of that for an International, the atmosphere is entirely different. A basic point of difference is that, whereas for an International the picnics are held in the car parks before the match, for the Sevens the picnics move into the ground itself. Invariably played in fine spring weather, the stands present a colourful vista of shirt-sleeves and summer dresses. From noon to

Bob Hiller's place-kicking concentration, in the strip of Harlequins, for whom Twickenham was so long their home ground.

nightfall it is a gala day of drinking and eating, strolling about to meet friends for a chat between rounds, and noisy, good-humoured cheering, clapping and booing of favourite teams and rivals on the field of play where the players are trying to outdo one another in self-inflicted physical exhaustion in one of the most masochistic forms of sport ever thought up.

Chapter 10

Twickenham's Famous Bath Tubs

Apart from those privileged to be Internationals and others who have played at Twickenham at lower levels, few people have ever been in the dressing-rooms. On the day of a big match a close guard is kept at the two entrances under the West Stand and, as one International put it, 'we are sealed off from intruders'. With rare exceptions the only non-participants allowed into the dressing-rooms are the selectors, the coach, the team doctor and the Secretary of the RFU. Even after the game wives, girl friends, male friends and other well-wishers must wait without.

The two dressing-rooms are labelled above each door Room 1 (England's) and Room 2, but this is merely the designation when there is nothing happening at Twickenham. When a game is on it is a nice little touch at a ground where they pride themselves on such niceties that the 'Room 1' and 'Room 2' panels are taken out of the slots and the names of the two teams of the day inserted, the hand-painted lettering being in the colours of each team concerned. The Harlequins' sign is of rainbow beauty. Naturally these get souvenired regularly and the powers-that-be at Twickenham just shrug their shoulders good-naturedly and tell the paint shop, under the North Stand, to get cracking on replacements.

Each dressing-room has a main large room with enough wall benches and clothes hooks to accommodate two or more teams. Adjoining this is an even larger room containing showers and what might be termed a distinctive feature of the Twickenham dressing-rooms – the huge bathtubs (seven in the England dressing-room and, for no known reason, eight in the visitors') instead of the communal bath used at most rugby grounds. Standing unadorned in their utilitarian splendour, each bath is big enough to accommodate a player and a friend. No 16-stone forward, no matter how lanky, has ever had cause for complaint about the solid comfort and sheer joy of soaking in one of these

Twickenham's Famous Bath Tubs

massive tubs after a match. In fact, when the Rugby Union, thinking that these baths of 1931 vintage could well be replaced by one modern communal bath, sounded out the players they universally replied that if that were done it would be depriving them of one of Twickenham's great attractions.

The teams arrive in the dressing-rooms an hour before the big game, this being generally accepted as just the right amount of time – no more, no less – in which to change, talk tactics, make use if need be of the massage table or the doctor's thoroughly equipped surgery across the hall, and to get themselves in just the right frame of mind for events to come.

Although sealed off, some of the sound effects of the big occasion permeate through to them. They can hear the chatter of the throng in the West Concourse between the car park and the back of the stand where, as O. L. Owen once put it, 'old friends and acquaintances foregather at what for long has ranked among the famous meeting places of the world'. And as one of the more lyrical of the internationals phrased it, 'draughts of music float through to us from the band on the pitch'.

Twenty minutes before kick-off there are the team photos, always by tradition taken out on the field just by the tunnel exit with a bit of the North Stand in the background. There are two schools of thought about this photographic session. Many of the players welcome it as a help in counteracting those butterflies within, getting the flavour of the ground and the crowd. Others do not like it because they have the feeling of being all dressed up and nowhere to go. The latter school of thought sometimes wins. The All Blacks before their match with the Barbarians in 1974, for example, refused to go out for a group shot. In the same year both Oxford and Cambridge said they were not interested when all was set up for the pictures.

Players will tell you that when they trot out on to the field the roar of the crowd seems to hit them right in the face but once the game is under way they are never really conscious of crowd noises. Concentration on the matter at hand makes them oblivious to it. And despite how much the radio and TV commentators deplore those catcalls that can sometimes be heard when a place-kicker is running up to kick, the players concerned say that it does not really affect them. They are deaf to such things in their determination to get that ball up between the posts.

Each England player is issued with a numbered jersey, a pair of stockings and a track suit, which he may keep. Shorts and boots he provides himself, since they are a more personal matter, particularly the boots, about which rugby players – at all levels of the game – are justifiably fussy. Fleet-footed wings and locks naturally go for a different type of boot. Place-kickers have their treasured pair, the ones they were wearing in that match in which they just could not miss, and are in hopes that it will happen again. For example, that greatest place-kicker of them all, Don Clarke, used to deposit with his gear in the dressing-room before a match what he called his 'boots for stealing', a useless old pair which were expendable, his lucky boots being kept securely locked in his car to be donned just before kick-off.

The replacements for an England International match also are each issued with a jersey, stockings and track suit. But if they do not take the field, reluctantly these have to be handed back after the game. Which makes sense, since it would hardly be right for someone to be able proudly to display his England jersey if in fact he never actually participated. The substitutes are issued also with superb woollen rugs which anyone – rugby player or not – would love to possess, but these, too, have to be handed back, being merely to keep them warm while sitting in the stand until such time as they may have excitedly mixed feelings at seeing one of their team mates being carried from the field.

Les Rose, of the Twickenham staff, who since 1947 has been looking after the jersey situation among other things, has learned from experience so that when the England side trot out on to the pitch in their jerseys numbered 1 to 15 there are no obvious misfits. The range of sizes 42 to 46 is the general rule of thumb to cover everything from scrum-half to line-out giant, although he has to be constantly wary of a Coughtrie appearing on the scene.

Invariably a player will keep his first England jersey – forever! – but if lucky enough to be chosen again he will start swapping, to confuse innocent bystanders at a training session by appearing as an All Black or a Springbok. The RFU does insist on the England track suit being brought along to those sessions, in case there is a picture to be taken and some sort of uniform look is required, but apart from that the players are not issued with special gear for practices. A Lions team was once kitted out in a distinctive stripe for training but it never caught on. It was too drastic a departure from the traditional motley collection of faded, torn, ill-fitting club, county and International jerseys that make any squad session such a colourful occasion.

Under the West Stand there is a cupboard just by the tunnel exit where the balls are kept. On the shelves a batch of greyish-looking used balls for training sessions stood out in sharp contrast to two light tan, virginal 'Match' balls as supplied by James Gilbert Ltd, of Rugby, inventors of the rugby football as we know it today. I saw these just before an International match and was told that they were the balls for the big match. 'May I?' I asked. 'Certainly', they said and I felt privileged to be able to pick one of them up, examine the beautiful hand-made workmanship and get that wonderful smell of fine leather. And as I handled it I could not help but be reminded of that well-known Bill McLaren cliché, trotted out whenever the ball goes to either full-back at the start of a game – 'He'll be thankful for that early feel of the ball.'

At the big rugby grounds abroad they have long used three balls for a match, with ball-boys, since so many of them are cricket fields as well and otherwise it would so often be a long wait at line-outs. The same sort of arrangement applies at Cardiff Arms Park where that ghastly dog track means that the ball drifts off to open spaces around the playing area. But at Twickenham, where spectators are positioned so close to the playing area and are ever willing to toss the ball back on to the field when it drops among them, only one is needed, with a spare in case anything should go amiss.

Rarely does the spare ball come into use. One occasion on which it did was not without its amusing aspect. It was the England–Wales match of 1960 and one of Don Rutherford's two penalties landed among a group of Welsh supporters on the South Terrace. This time it was not tossed back on to the field.

What happened was that a quick-thinking Welshman whipped the pin out of his rosette and punctured the ball. He shoved the deflated leather up under his coat and then, with every appearance of innocence, joined the unsuccessful hunt for the missing ball. The spare one had to be brought on so that the game could be resumed. The lost ball was not seen again until the following morning when, inflated once more, it was put on display at the engineering works where the Welshman was employed – with 'The One That Got Away', the title of a current film, inscribed on it. However, it did not stay on show for long. A local Detective-Inspector named Davies, a former Llanelli forward, admitted that he was rather a spoil-sport but said that technically it was a theft and the stolen property was returned to Twickenham. But no charge was laid.

By tradition both balls for a big match at Twickenham 'disappear' after the game, but to be fair to both sides they see to it that they disappear in the direction of the two opposing captains.

Chapter 11

A Notable First

By the middle of the 1930s, England supporters could look back on the rather poor record of their side against the touring teams from below the equator, who had started their visits in 1888.

Certainly England had beaten that swashbuckling first touring team, generally called 'The Maoris', and a band of New South Welshmen under the name of the Waratahs had been conclusively disposed of in 1928. But against the major sides – the All Blacks, the Springboks and the Wallabies – they had never been able to score a victory.

But in 1936 they were to record a notable first. And not only was it notable for being England's first win against the southern giants. It produced what many people regard as the greatest individual try ever scored at Twickenham.

OBOLENSKY'S MATCH
England v. New Zealand, 4 January 1936

I certainly picked a good one for the first International I ever watched at Twickenham.

If I may be excused a personal digression to set the scene, I had come over as an enthusiastic young correspondent with the Third All Blacks on their tour of the British Isles. I say enthusiastic because all New Zealanders expected great things of this team. Their predecessors in 1924–5 had swept the board, winning every match they played, and they were expected to carry on from where the Invincibles had left off.

They lost their fifth match, against Swansea. Just how shattering a blow that was you would not realise unless you were aware of how seriously New Zealanders take their rugby. They were castigated for this terrible thing they had done and morale within the team plummeted. Management did not help. The manager of the side was Mr V. R. S. Meredith KC, Crown Prosecutor back in Auckland, a man who had the faculty of making anybody who came into contact

A picture to make hat manufacturers weep for the good old days. Among spectators crowded into the newly extended South Terrace in 1930 not more than a dozen are to be seen without headgear. Note scoreboard and clock at the back – all right for those in the stands to see but a crick in the neck for those on the terrace.

with him feel like a badgered witness. The captain was Jack Manchester, who was built like a giant oak.

As the tour progressed and it was seen that they were far below the standard set by their forerunners, the management became increasingly resentful of criticism, and any member of the press party who indulged in it was likely to find his mail on the floor of the team room with 'Not known' scrawled across it. I was placed in a rather awkward position since the paper for which I was covering the tour was not known for throwing its money around but was very well known for colourful presentation of news. The outcome was that I had to write my reports in the tightest, most economical form of cable and this they expanded freely into graphic prose. In one match report when adjudging the performance of the burly forward Hugh McLean, brother of rugby writer T. P. ('Happy') McLean, I cabled: MCLEAN PLAYED UNWELL. This appeared in the paper as 'McLean trundled around the field like a tired elephant'. In view of the climate of resentment against criticism that sort of remark could have turned into a nasty business when a clipping reached the team from New Zealand.

These All Blacks were held to a draw by Ulster and then they did something absolutely unforgivable. They were beaten by Wales. This was just before what was undoubtedly the most miserable Christmas any touring party has had to get through and then, after managing to fend off London Counties on Boxing Day, the final game of the tour in which they had better go out in a blaze of glory unless they wanted to be thrown into the steaming mud pools of Rotorua on their return – the match against England at Twickenham.

The teams:

England: H. G. Owen-Smith (Oxford, St Mary's H); A. Obolensky (Oxford), P. Cranmer (Oxford), R. A. Gerrard (Bath), H. S. Sever (Sale); P. L. Candler (Cambridge, Barts), B. C. Gadney (Leicester, capt.); D. A. Kendrew (Leicester), E. S. Nicholson (Oxford), R. J. Longland (Northampton), C. S. H. Webb (Devonport S), A. J. Clarke (Coventry), E. A. Hamilton-Hill (Harlequins), P. E. Dunkley (Harlequins), W. H. Weston (Northampton).

New Zealand: G. Gilbert; N. Ball, C. J. Oliver, N. Mitchell; T. H. C. Caughey, E. W. Tindill; M. N. Corner; A. Lambourn, W. E. Hadley, J. Hore, J. E. Manchester (capt.), R. R. King, S. T. Reid, H. F. McLean, A. Mahoney.

Referee: J. W. Faull.

The attendance of 73,000 was a record for Twickenham and the excitement of the match for the crowd was not that of seeing the lead taken by one team then the other, with the result in doubt right up to the final whistle. It was the sheer joy of seeing England doing something unique – completely outclassing a major touring side and in the course of that one of their players making his name ever remembered by scoring two superb tries, the second of which is arguably the best ever scored at Twickenham.

Prince Alexander Obolensky, variously nicknamed 'Obo' and the Flying Slav, had been born in St Petersburg in 1916 and was brought out of Russia to England at the time of the Bolshevik Revolution in the following year. He went to Kent College in Canterbury and then on to Brasenose at Oxford, where he won the first of his two Blues in 1935. The All Blacks already knew the capabilities of the tall, blond, long-striding winger. In their match against Oxford he had given them a scare when, with the score merely 5–4 in their favour, he had rounded off a back movement with a brilliant run to score under the posts and make them 5–9 in arrears. They only just prevented it from being the winning try by scrambling a score in the corner in the dying minutes and their full-back, Gilbert, saving the day with the necessary two points for victory.

It was his first outing for England in this match at Twickenham which started with New Zealand exerting some determined pressure. First the loose forward Tori Reid (whose first name sounded appropriately Maori but was in fact short for what his parents had oddly christened him – Sanatorium) was on hand after a break by Gilbert coming into the line and was only just forced into touch by Owen-Smith. Then Caughey, the centre, broke through and was going well until shatteringly tackled jointly by Cranmer and Gerrard. And after a vigorous forward rush from half way King actually did cross the line, only to be called back by the touch judge's flag three yards out.

Then suddenly the whole scene changed dramatically. From England possession at a midfield scrum Gadney missed out his fly-half and sent direct to Cranmer. He transferred to his co-centre Gerrard, who timed his pass nicely to Obolensky on the right wing with forty yards to go. Having beaten his opposite number, Ball, and the full-back Gilbert in the Oxford game, he proceeded to do the same thing again. This time, however, it was a much longer run-in and he finished by his corner flag for what could have been the try of the match, had he not elected to be even more spectacular later. Dunkley's conversion attempt hit the crossbar and bounced back. England 3, New Zealand 0.

England were playing towards the North Stand, so that when, just before half-time, Obolensky scored the try that rugby fans are still talking about we in the press box in the centre of the East Stand were in the perfect position to observe what happened since we were in effect looking over his shoulder when he got the ball and summed up the situation in front of him.

The move started in very much the same way as the previous one – from a scrum near midfield just inside the All Blacks' half. The England backs were aligned to the right – Gadney, Candler, Cranmer, Gerrard, Obolensky – but this time Gadney did not skip Candler. The ball went conventionally from Gadney to Candler to Cranmer, who made a break and when challenged by the cover defence passed inside to Candler. The New Zealand defenders, bearing in mind Obolensky's previous try in the corner, were converging over to his wing. From our vantage point in the press box behind Obolensky we could see precisely what he caught sight of – a channel through them over to the other corner flag. He ran infield around the outside centre, Gerrard, and was on hand to take Candler's pass at the same spot forty yards out from which he had set off for his first try. The two men immediately in front of him, scrum-half Merv Corner, who had been doing some energetic corner-flagging, and his opposing wing, Ball, were completely outwitted when they continued their progress towards Obolensky's touchline to cut him off, only to realise suddenly that he was not making the same trip. He was hell bent on a diagonal run over to the other corner.

For a frozen moment there was the picture: Obolensky getting into full stride with his scrum-half Gadney and left wing Sever outside him and the entire New Zealand defence wrong-footed, swirling around to set off in pursuit.

Even the New Zealand right wing, Mitchell, had been rushing across the field to help prevent what the All Blacks all thought was going to be an attempt by Obolensky to repeat his first try, so that when the two met ten yards out from the goal line the New Zealander was off balance. He was left floundering as Obolensky swerved around him to record that oddity in International rugby – a right wing's try scored in the left wing's preserve.

Half-time: England 6, New Zealand 0.

Six points down was not the end of the world and the All Blacks went into all-out attack in the second half. Hadley, their hooker, nearly got over. Mitchell was stopped on the line. England's tackling was magnificent and the New Zealanders seemed to despair of finding any way through her defence. Tindill and then Gilbert took long-range potshots at goal, both of which went astray. Then, when Cranmer showed them how to do it, with his left foot, and England were 10–0 up the heart seemed to go right out of the tourists. England were playing with confidence, sure on defence and inventive on attack. Cranmer sliced through their backline again and sent Sever away to evade two

'Obo' the Flying Slav, otherwise Prince Alexander Obolensky, shown here in a Rosslyn Park jersey, the England right wing who scored one of Twickenham's greatest ever tries against the 1935–6 All Blacks.

tackles and score under the posts. Even that easy conversion was missed but the final score of 13–0 was the worst defeat New Zealand had suffered in her rugby history.

Apologists for the All Blacks said that they were jaded, the players were 'over-played and stale . . . the tour was finishing, football had lost its glamour . . . their resoluteness, fire and dash had been sapped by many matches'. But if that were the case why had the same thing not applied to the All Blacks in 1925 on their tour of the same length when they had beaten England in the final match? To adopt such an attitude was unfair to this 1936 England side, who made the tourists look irresolute and lacking in dash because they outclassed them.

According to a contemporary report 'the final whistle was greeted by the crowd with a deafening roar' in acknowledgement of what even today stands as by far the biggest and most convincing win by any of the Home Countries over either of those overseas giants, the All Blacks and the Springboks. On the field at the end, the report continued, 'the New Zealanders foregathered with their victorious opponents, handshaking was going on everywhere, Manchester was congratulating Gadney, and Ball was seen slapping Prince Obolensky on the back'. As well he might, it could be added.

After that dramatic debut for England, Obolensky played in the remaining three Internationals of the season but that, oddly enough, was the end of his career in big-time rugby. He played for Rosslyn Park when he came down from Oxford but was never again picked for England. He became a Pilot Officer with the RAF and was the first rugby International to be killed in World War II, meeting his death in a flying training accident in Norfolk.

Chapter 12

Royal Occasions

Of the five monarchs (Edward VII, George V, Edward VIII, George VI and Elizabeth II) who have been on the throne since Twickenham opened, the one who could be said to have been the greatest rugby fan was George V. Apart from the annual formal visit, he used to like to come just to watch rugby. With his keen sense of humour he used to delight in getting the staff at Twickenham on the hop by having an equerry phone the ground out of the blue on the morning of a match and say: 'His Majesty is coming to the game this afternoon.' Great scurrying around to get out the red carpet.

Someone on the staff of those days thought it would improve his comfort in the Royal Box if something could be rigged up to offset the fact that sometimes rain can drift in to that part of the stand. So a panel of glass was installed in the parapet in front of the royal seat with an attachment whereby it could be raised if need be, like winding up a car window. One windy wet day the drizzle did indeed start to drift in and the contraption was brought into use. But not for long. The man who had installed it had not thought in terms of a windscreen-wiper and in no time His Majesty had announced forcibly: 'I can't see what on earth's going on, will somebody remove this bloody thing!'

The Royal Box is situated in front of the committee box in the centre of the lower West Stand, best seats in the house, as they should be. The seats of themselves are not the same wooden tip-up variety spectators are accustomed to. The Royal Box when not in use is just a bare stretch of concrete there above the players' tunnel and the red-painted wicker armchairs are stored away out of the elements until such time as they are needed. There are twenty of them and on a wall in the President's Room is a plaque headed 'The Royal Box' with twenty slots on it into which are put the names of the members of the royal party so that they will know where they will be sitting. The original Royal Box plaque used to hang free on the wall but it unaccountably disappeared and this new one is securely screwed down.

Besides the choice position of the Royal Box and the comfort of the

Most ardent royal rugby fan was George V, here meeting the England side of 1928. Fifth from left is the great centre Carl Aarvold, now an eminent judge. England strip seemed difficult to keep whiter than white in those days before detergents, and players were casual about socks to the extent of wearing golf stockings.

easy chairs, another amenity is a large hot water pipe which runs along its entire length at the base of the parapet in front – the only form of central heating provided for the viewing public at Twickenham, which again is as it should be.

The Secretary of the RFU, Air Commodore Weighill, sits at one end of the Royal Box and by his side is a push button which he brings into use when the Queen is about to emerge from below to take her place in the stand. It turns on a little red light in front of the box, which is the signal for the bandmaster down on the field to scrub *Orpheus in the Underworld* or whatever the band happen to be playing and launch into the National Anthem.

As well as the formal visit each year by Her Majesty, Patron of the Rugby Football Union, there are visits to Twickenham by other members of the Royal Family and one that stays in the mind was the occasion of the charity match between England and France in 1974 following the air disaster outside Paris. A big crowd had supported this fund-raising game and Princess Alexandra and her family were present. No one who was there will ever forget the half-time diversion when a young man in the crowd decided to have a go at the then popular craze of streaking. Taking all his clothes off and leaving them in the care of a friend, he sprinted right across the field, to the surprise of everybody at first, then to gales of laughter. Since his streak was from the East Stand to the arms of the law in front of the West Stand,

Crown Prince and Princess of Japan pay a visit in 1935. Extreme left is Dr Jimmy Russell-Cargill, who started Middlesex Sevens in 1926, and the grey haired gentleman (centre) is Billy Williams.

A royal occasion in 1936, with two kings present, both of whom were forced to resign. Edward VIII can easily be spotted and two away from him on his right is King Farouk, of all people.

An attractive shot of the Queen at the Middlesex Sevens in 1951, with Lord Wakefield, President of the RFU that year.

the view from the Royal Box was, not to put too fine a point on it, fully frontal. Air Commodore Weighill, who was sitting with Princess Alexandra's youngsters, reported that they thought it was a huge joke. The reaction of Her Highness, it being a rather delicate matter, was not recorded.

The most hilarious part of this incident, of course, was the performance of one of the coppers, who used his helmet to restore propriety, which provided one of the best and most reprinted action pictures ever taken at Twickenham. It was a *Daily Mirror* front-page scoop and it became so famous that the Rugby Union decided that it would make a really out of the ordinary Christmas card – until they had second thoughts. A pity.

The aftermath was that the streaker got a £10 fine in the magistrate's court, the magistrate not being nearly as imaginative as the one in New Zealand when a similar thing happened. The magistrate out there asked the streaker why he had done it and upon being told, 'I want to be seen!', he said: 'All right, make a contribution of $50 to the Blind Institute and when you bring me the receipt you can go free.'

The late Duke of Gloucester, brother of George VI, was keen not only on rugby itself but on all aspects of the game. An Army man, he took much interest in the Inter-Services matches, went to them regularly and never felt it necessary to hurry home when the after-match activities got under way at the bar.

The official annual royal visit is invariably for the Calcutta Cup when the Rugby Union is host for the fixture. Twickenham has no royal cup presentation as Wembley does for soccer's FA Cup and Rugby League's Challenge Cup. Many rugby followers feel that the Calcutta Cup would afford a good opportunity for Twickenham to have the same sort of thing. The Rugby Union, however, has never felt that it would fit into the Twickenham syndrome. A pity in some ways, for at least it would give rugby fans a chance to get a sight of the trophy of which they have heard so much and which so few people have ever seen. The RFU and the Scottish Rugby Union safeguard it in a manner which would seem to go far beyond its intrinsic value of £60.

THE INNER SANCTUM

It is given to few ever to have the pleasure of being in the Royal Box. But there is also another part of Twickenham by no means open to the general public and in this respect the ground differs radically from Lord's.

At Lord's the holy of holies – the pavilion – is not all that holy. The thousands of MCC and Middlesex members and their friends, members of the visiting club playing there – a high percentage of the males of any crowd at Lord's know what it is like to be in the pavilion. But in contrast how many spectators at Twickenham can say that they know what it is like in the equivalent at rugby's headquarters – the committee rooms under the West Stand?

The *sanctum santorum* is approached by a broad panelled staircase lined with framed photographs of Royalty at Twickenham. In the lobby at the top of the stairs is a large glass showcase in which are displayed (on match days) the interesting gifts presented to the Rugby Football Union by other Unions and clubs all over the world on the occasion of the centenary in 1971 and at other times during its history. Interesting and valuable, they are securely locked away in the vaults when there is no match.

From the lobby you can go straight on and emerge in the committee box on the half way line in the lower West Stand accommodation. But what guest would want to take his seat right away when there are such good pre-match facilities to be enjoyed?

To the left of the lobby is the large, L-shaped committee lounge. A bar, of course, and food available but once that sort of thing has been taken care of, it is fascinating to look around at all the wall decorations. There are two huge oil paintings of rugby in Victorian times by W. B. Woollan, one of a Yorkshire and Lancashire match and the other, which hung on the line in the Royal Academy in 1879, depicts a game between Cambridge University and, it is thought, Newport, although nobody is quite certain. These paintings are so big as to be like murals and apart from them the interesting thing is that everything else on display has been placed well above head height, so that they can still be viewed in the crush that develops in the lounge on match days.

Up near the ceiling there is a colourful frieze of plaques bearing the crests of rugby clubs which are more than a hundred years old and any club which celebrates its centenary has the privilege of joining this array. Equally colourful is the large County Championship board which records all the winners since Yorkshire were declared first champions in 1889. A springbok head securely screwed to the wall looks down upon the assembled committee members and their guests. It was the one which London Counties won from the 1951–2 Springboks with their memorable 11–9 victory which was the single setback which prevented the tourists from returning home unconquered.

At the other side of the lobby is the President's Room, smaller than the committee lounge but more opulently furnished, as befits the fact that it is here that the President of the Rugby Union entertains

Although barely related to rugby, this award-winning photograph is probably the most published picture ever to come out of Twickenham. The occasion was the 1974 charity match between England and France.

Royalty, the Prime Minister and other dignitaries when they are guests at a match at Twickenham.

Next door is the Committee Room reserved exclusively for committee members of the RFU and visiting rugby unions.

From one wall a portrait of Her Majesty the Queen, watches over them and on the other walls are pictures of every President since the first, Algernon Rutter, of Richmond, to the incumbent at the time of writing, G. Tarn Bainbridge. In this distinguished company there is one who never attained the presidency but whose portrait is present for a special reason. After all Twickenham Rugby Ground as such would never have come into being had it not been for Billy Williams.

Chapter 13

The Link between Rugby and Beer

At the original Twickenham there was one refreshment room. Today there are twenty permanent bars and on big match days twelve additional outlets for the sale of take-away drinks. This means that roughly speaking if you circle the ground you cannot go more than twenty paces without encountering somewhere to get a drink. This without a shadow of doubt makes Twickenham's facilities for alcoholic refreshment the most concentrated of any sports ground in Britain. In the world?

By way of comparison there are no bars at all for the public at Cardiff Arms Park, Murrayfield or Lansdowne Road. At Lord's Cricket Ground, where one would have thought that the hot summer sun or the need to fill in time when rain holds up play would be much more conducive to thirst slaking, there are merely half the number of bars that there are at Twickenham. At Wembley Stadium, with its capacity of more than 100,000, there are but sixteen.

The high point of Twickenham beer consumption comes at the end of the season on the day of the Middlesex Sevens. No fewer than 50,000 pints are downed during that tournament. As a yardstick to measure what a flooding intake that is, a busy pub would be very pleased to get rid of 1,000 pints in a day. On International days at Twickenham the figure is not as high, obviously. Such fixtures do not go on as long as the Sevens, with its numerous long intervals during which spectators can stroll to the bars, and at an International there is that 80-minute interruption to drinking time when people tend to be exclusively interested in what is happening on the field. Which means that an International crowd only manages to put away about half the quantity – a mere 3,000 gallons.

At the beginning of the 1974–5 season a horrifying rumour went around that the Rugby Union had decided that the bars at Twickenham would be closed for Internationals. It was said that this was the

The weather vane which replaced the scoreboard and clock at the back of the South Terrace in 1950. Designed by Kenneth Dalgleish, it depicts Hermes, the winged messenger, giving a well-directed pass.

Pre-match high-jinks at Twickenham in 1958 by a contingent from a quite well known rugby playing country.

result of complaints from spectators about hordes of young fans spilling out of the bars at kick-off time loaded internally and laden with great 'party-cans' of beer to continue their drinking, to the annoyance of those around. Also, it was said, householders in the Whitton Road had complained of after-match drinkers at the ground being quite unable to steer a straight course to the station and falling into hedges on the way, not to mention prize roses in the front gardens rotting at the roots through over-watering. Rumour had it that the Rugby Union had bowed to the complainants.

It transpired, however, that it had all been a ghastly error. A news agency report had got things garbled. A decision to restrict drinking at the ground had been misinterpreted as a total ban.

Up to the latter part of the 1960s Twickenham had been 'wide open' on big match days from noon until around 8 p.m. The early start was primarily for those who wished to have a drink with their lunch at the mobile canteens dotted around the ground or at one of the five permanent restaurants, each of which, incidentally, has its own bar in addition to the twenty already mentioned, but they are simply for those who have the formal lunch or tea at the ground. The late closing was for the convenience of those who wanted to make a real outing of their day at Twickenham.

When there is a big match on at Twickenham the clubs of London and its environs play their matches in the morning, to leave their members and supporters free to go to the big game. Not unnaturally they go in batches from this club and that club. Michael Green, undoubtedly the funniest writer about rugby, once told of a young man being dispatched by his club mates on the terraces just before the final whistle to dash out to the deserted West Bar, where the barmaids were having a last-minute cigarette before the big rush, and saying: 'Eighty pints of bitter, please.' Green pointed out that if this might sound outlandish it was not sufficient to make the barmaids look surprised. After all, it made sense. The beer would be lined up on the trestle tables outside the bar and when the match finished and as his party of twenty or so arrived they could each drink their three or four pints at leisure without having to battle through the scrum at the bar every time they wanted a refill.

The after-match highjinks, to the accompaniment of rugby songs and including such things as stripping in the rafters, used to continue well into the hours of darkness, for which reason it was seen fit to light bonfires, which could always be put out with the readily available fire extinguisher possessed by every man.

A time came, however, when the authorities felt that traditionally accepted antics of rugger types were getting out of hand.

Local publicans were complaining but not as one might have thought because they felt that the bars at the ground were taking business away from them. What they were unhappy about was that by the time the revellers reeled away from the ground and headed for the nearest local they were hardly the type of customers that publicans welcome with open arms.

Apart from anything else, keeping open late was felt to be uneconomic by those who do the catering for Twickenham. This is the well-known firm of Ring & Brymer, food and drink organisers for many of the biggest sports fixtures in Britain, who have had the Twickenham concession since 1926. They knew from experience that the bulk of the eating and drinking at an International is finished by six o'clock and to stay open after that merely for the relatively small coterie of solid drinkers was really not worth it by the time breakages and other wear and tear on the facilities were totted up.

Ring & Brymer have found that their complete stock of glasses at Twickenham, through breakages and theft, has to be replaced each season. They tried plastic mugs but it took only two Internationals for the 10,000 they put into use to disappear. A drawback was that these were a beautifully produced replica of the traditional pub pint with a handle and, as such, just the thing for souveniring. Much lighter than glass, batches of them could be hidden under the overcoat of a departing spectator, to solve all his problems of glasses for parties at home. One young man who was stopped at the gates was found to have no fewer than fifty secreted on his person, which is understood to be a record.

So, all things being considered, the RFU at the start of the 1974-5 season ordained some restrictions. Henceforth at the big matches the bars would shut a quarter of an hour before kick-off and remain closed throughout the progress of the game. At the final whistle they would open again for an hour. It remains to be seen in the years to come how closely these strictures will be adhered to among the ardent habitués of the huge barn-like bars of Twickenham.

In pre-war days when only one in thirty in Britain owned a car compared to one in five today naturally the bulk of the crowd went by train and to offer them hospitality after their short journey from the metropolis there were three pubs clustered around Twickenham station. One could step straight out of the station into the Albany. At the end of the little street that led up from the station to the main road leading from the centre of town to the ground stood the Railway Tavern and across the railway bridge was Rugby House with one bar at road level and two more down by the 'up' platform of the station.

However, in 1953 there was a radical change. The station, which had always been on the side of the bridge away from London, was moved to the near side. This was indeed a blow to the Albany. All of a sudden, from having the best location of the three it had the worst. Isolated over on the other side of the bridge, it was no longer on the route to the ground. The old match-day regulars of the Albany of course kept using it as their rendezvous but much of the valuable 'passing trade' was lost.

Then came another change. The narrow bridge, which carried all the traffic coming and going on that side of town, was proving inade-

The Link between Rugby and Beer

Spectacular loose forward and Wales captain, Alun Pask, goes over for the match-winning try against England in 1966, the year in which the majority of British supporters were unhappy that he was passed over for captaincy of the Lions in Australasia.

quate, so it was decided to replace it with a dual carriageway. This was opened in 1964 and as part of the scheme the old Rugby House lost its prominent position at one end of the old bridge and became somewhat hidden away on the corner of a large new office block.

The pub which came out best from the deal was the Railway Tavern, for it was now the only one of the three which could be clearly seen from the station on big match days. Early in the 1970s, to make it further attractive to the rugby clientele, it was given a face-lift and a change of name to the Cabbage Patch, which was the original nickname of the rugby ground. The main bar is furnished in Edwardian opulence – red plush wall seats, crystal chandeliers, potted palms – and what used to be the public bar is now, for no accountable reason, the Luverly War Bar, complete with World War I pictures on the walls, including a splendid portrayal of a young lady seeing her officer boyfriend off to the Front – 'For England, Home and Beauty'.

But it is not in these surroundings that the Twickhamists do their drinking. On the day of an International it is action stations at the Cabbage Patch. Everything is cleared out – the chairs and tables, potted palms, war pictures, anything movable – and the place is left bare so that (a) there is maximum room for the shoulder-to-shoulder drinkers and (b) things do not get thrown around.

No less than 230 gallons of beer will be consumed before the end of the day and more than 300 glasses lost, stolen or broken. John Blaylock, who manages the pub with his wife, Janis, has a special staff to go hunting for glasses in the streets and alleyways in the immediate vicinity. In fact he has more people employed collecting glasses than serving drinks. 'It's worth it', he will tell you.

Not by any means are these three and the other pubs in Twickenham itself the only ones frequented by fans before and after the big match.

The Duke of Cambridge, opposite the entrance gates to Kneller Hall, is popular with many and obviously it was ideally sited for the military trumpeters and trombonists to whip out and wet their whistles between sessions, long before it became a favourite rendezvous for Twickenham fans.

The London Apprentice on the Thames at Isleworth, with its 450 years of history of boys working on the river, is another popular meeting place; the Jolly Gardener, the Harlequin at Mogden Lane – ever since Twickenham opened pubs such as these have been handed down from father to son as places for spectators to meet up ('See you at the Balmy Arms!') before going in groups to the match.

There is a whole batch of them in Richmond. The White Swan in a lane leading down from Richmond Green to the river is popular with the Rosslyn Park crowd and so jampacked does it become that mine host John Foster will tell you that at the beginning of each season the more sedate of his customers ask him for the Twickenham fixture list so that they can tick off the dates of the Internationals as days on which to be elsewhere.

Two of the Richmond pubs which have a big advantage over the others are the Orange Tree, near the station, and the White Cross, on the river a couple of hundred yards from Richmond Bridge. Both of these serve the brand of beer acknowledged as far and away Britain's best brew.

Richmond club players, as a change from their own free-flowing bars at Athletic Park, meet up at the Sun. There are also the Watermen's Arms, the Ship, the Angel and Crown, the Britannia, the Prince's Head . . .

This most certainly is not a complete list of the pubs that play such a great part in making an International at Twickenham the great day's outing that it is.

Chapter 14

When Scotland Did Not Disappoint

In International rugby in modern times it often seems to be the main role of Scotland to disappoint. She has produced great players in recent years – Ken Scotland, H. F. McLeod, Rollo, A. R. Smith, Stewart Wilson, Hinshelwood, Telfer, Laidlaw, Frame, Chisholm and Hastie, the brothers P. C. and Gordon Brown, through to 'Mighty Mouse' McLauchlan. And at the outset of practically every season the general feeling is that 'this will be Scotland's year'. But something always seems to go wrong. Not once in the postwar era has Scotland managed to win the championship outright.

One has to go way back to 1938 to find the last time Scotland wound up at the top of the table. And what a great year it was – unbeaten, undisputed champions who were to finish off the International season with one of the truly great Calcutta Cup matches at Twickenham.

SHAW'S MATCH
England v. Scotland, 19 March 1938

Some years ago a middle-aged Scotsman of my acquaintance who was a great enthusiast of the game was talking rugby with me when the name of R. Wilson Shaw cropped up. 'Ah!' he said, all his national pride welling up within him. 'I was there at Twickenham when he scored that marvellous try. I can see the little chap now, bobbing and weaving his way through the England team and leaving them standing.'

There was a crowd of 70,000 at Twickenham but far more people than that saw the match live, for this was one of the first Internationals ever televised. The privileged television viewers did not have to wait to go to a cinema in the following week to see the highlights on Movietone News, which up till then had been the only way for those not at a match to see any of the action.

The marvellous try, of course, was the one Wilson Shaw scored just

Scotland scrum-half Dougie Morgan is felled by Stack Stevens in the 1973 England–Scotland match, with varied reactions from team-mates Strachan, McHarg, MacEwan and Gordon Brown.

as the referee was about to whistle up full time in the Calcutta Cup match of 19 March 1938, a try which not only put the result of the match beyond doubt but was also the most spectacular way possible of bringing to a climax a golden year for Scotland in which they won the Championship, the Triple Crown and the Calcutta Cup, a feat which their faithful followers are still hopefully waiting for them to repeat.

At the time I was talking to my Scottish friend I was working on a rugby book in which were included great moments of the game described by the players who had engineered them. Naturally I decided to get in touch with Shaw and ask him to recall that try for the book. I received a curt letter back from him: 'It was all a long time ago. Nobody is interested now.'

I know he had the reputation of being modest in the extreme but I thought that attitude was just a little bit stuffy. Every sport must have its heroes and Shaw was quite inaccurate in saying that nobody is interested now. Denis Compton, Stanley Matthews, W. W. Wakefield – no matter how far back you go people *are* interested, otherwise why would I happen upon my younger son at our mini-cricket pitch in the garden with a book open on a deck-chair, consulting it and then saying to me: 'Watch! See if I bowl like Wilfred Rhodes.'

So, in the absence of a first-hand report from Wilson Shaw on what came to be regarded among the greatest Calcutta Cup matches, one can only do one's best.

It must have been a real thriller, not only being high-scoring in those defensive 1930s of single-figure results and nil-all draws, but also because of the way the lead fluctuated.

It was the last and key match of the Championship. An England win would have meant that they shared it with Wales and Scotland; a draw would have given it to Scotland but without the Triple Crown or the Calcutta Cup, currently held by England. So the Scots took the field dead set on victory and a clean sweep.

The teams were:

England: G. W. Parker (Blackheath); E. J. Unwin (Rosslyn Park), P. L. Candler (Barts), P. Cranmer (Moseley), H. S. Sever (Sale); F. J. Reynolds (Old Cranleighans), J. L. Giles (Coventry); R. J. Longland (Northampton), H. B. Toft (Waterloo, capt.), H. F. Wheatley (Coventry), R. M. Marshall (Oxford), A. Wheatley (Coventry), W. H. Weston (Northampton), D. L. K. Milman (Bedford), A. A. Brown (Exeter).

Scotland: G. Roberts (Watsonians); W. N. Renwick (London Scottish), R. C. S. Dick (Guy's), D. J. Macrae (St Andres's U), C. J. S. Forrest (Cambridge); R. W. Shaw (Glasgow HSFP, capt.), T. F. Dorward (Gala); W. F. Blackadder (West of Scotland), J. D. Hastie (Melrose), W. M. Inglis (Royal Engineers), G. B. Horsburgh (London Scottish), A. Roy (Waterloo), W. B. Young (Cambridge), P. L. Duff (Glasgow Academicals), W. H. Crawford (United Services).

Referee: I. David (Wales).

Shaw, then twenty-four years old, had been restored to the captaincy after considerable dithering by the Scottish selectors, who had appointed him captain in 1936 and in the next two seasons shared it around. However, this was not the only sort of indecision from which he suffered at their hands. At school, being small, he had automatically started at scrum-half but was gradually moved out along the backline to the wing when it was realised that he had a terrific turn of speed.

But when he left Glasgow High School and began playing for the Former Pupils it was felt that, since he was an elusive and brainy player, he was wasted on the wing. So it was at fly-half that he featured for the club and won his first cap in 1934. In due course, however, the Scottish selectors fell into the same mistake as his sports master at school and were tempted to make the most of his speed by playing him at centre or wing. How wasteful this was was indicated by the sigh of relief that was said to go up from his opponents in the other countries when Scotland teams were announced and it was seen that he was not being played at fly-half.

Playing now in his best position, Shaw gave every indication from the outset that he was going to dominate the game and make it undeniably his match. Within ten minutes he had set up the first try. Grahame Parker, who had just taken over as England's full-back after Owen-Smith had returned to South Africa, failed to gather a kick upfield and Shaw dashed in to snap up the ball. When he found himself blocked he sent out a beautifully judged kick to the corner flag which bounced right into the hands of Renwick, Oxford winger, following up. Scotland were against a strong wind, which sent the conversion attempt astray, but a couple of minutes later it was helpful for Parker to goal a long penalty and bring the scores level. Soon he was to make use of it again with another good kick and England were 6–3 up.

At the end of half an hour Scotland had come level again. England had been opting for scrums instead of line-outs, as was permitted in those days, and it was the logical thing to do in view of the presence in their front row of that great hooker H. B. Toft. At a scrum in their 25 he did his job but the ball did not come back cleanly and Renwick was able to snatch it and dive over for his second try. England 6, Scotland 6.

Shaw, in the words of a contemporary writer, 'was continually prodding, probing and racing free from his immediate opponents to worry Parker and the English deep coverers' and he was to initiate Scotland's next try. When possession for England, gained by Toft from a scrum, was again wasted, Shaw nipped in to link with his back-row forwards, the ball eventually finding its way out to the centres for Dick to score and make it 9–6 to Scotland.

Within two minutes, however, England's centres had retaliated. The two Peters, Cranmer and Candler, who had done such good service for England, were playing in what was to be the last International for each of them and when the fly-half, Reynolds, made a break they capitalised on it so effectively that Unwin on the wing was given a clear run in for a try.

The pace had been hectic and the fast open play a treat for the

Twickenham crowd. With half-time coming up 9-all seemed just the right time to take a breather. Shaw, however, decided to end the session with a flourish. He snatched the ball from the feet of the England forwards, evaded two tacklers and then with only Parker between him and the goal line swerved around him so devastatingly that it could have been a contributing factor to this being Parker's second and last appearance for England.

We are rather spoiled today as far as high-scoring matches are concerned. It is interesting that, when the interval came with Scotland leading 12–9, there was a hubbub of excitement in the crowd because more points had been scored in that first half than in the full eighty minutes of any International at Twickenham in the past five years.

It was not long into the second half that England kept the see-saw going by taking the lead again. Their forwards were giving the backs wonderful service, mainly through Toft completely outhooking his opposite number, but it was all being wasted through dropped passes, Cranmer being the main culprit. Then when the ball came back from a scrum yet again Reynolds seemed to despair of his outsides making good use of it and let fly with a drop kick, the four points of a drop goal in those days making it England 13, Scotland 12.

Scotland's place-kicker, the Navy forward W. H. Crawford, had contributed nothing in the first half but now with the wind behind him he switched the score around to 15–13 in Scotland's favour with a penalty and then to 18–13 with another. But England's Parker was not to be outdone. He kicked a beauty from a wide angle into the wind and with Scotland's lead cut to a mere two points the stage was set for a grandstand finish. There had not been a Calcutta Cup match as exciting since the opening of Murrayfield in 1925 when England's eventual 14–11 win had been in doubt right up to the last minute. The feeling now among the Twickhamists was that their side could pull it off again.

R. Wilson Shaw, however, frustrated them with what still ranks as one of the best individual tries ever seen at Twickenham.

When the ball went loose near half way he picked up and with his amazing ability apparently to reach full speed almost from take-off he set forth with what seemed to be the entire England side arrayed between him and the goal line. He dodged, weaved and swerved in and out among the white shirts and even the most partisan among the spectators could not help but join the ovation he got when his brilliance had clinched victory for Scotland 21–16 at the final whistle.

As a report at the time put it: 'There was no sadness in English hearts, because they had shared in a memorable occasion.'

And my Scottish friend, who had been watching the game from the other end of the field, recalled: 'I shall never forget the sight of that little figure in the blue jersey disappearing into the mist all on his own with the whole of the England team after him.'

Chapter 15

Getting the Picture

The telecasting of matches at Twickenham had started in that 1937-8 season to a select band of television-set owners, a minute percentage of the 10 to 12 million who tune in to the Internationals today. And of course those rugby television viewers in the 1930s were exclusively British, since this country was unique in the world at that time in having a television service. American television, for example, did not get going until the late 1940s.

Nowadays, of course, the televised Internationals at Twickenham, and the other British venues, find their way to all corners of the world and some mighty odd corners at that. If one needed proof that rugby is a booming sport one need only look at the unexpected countries which seek facilities from the BBC to tune into the Internationals and the other big games.

An example of this was the excitedly awaited clash between the Barbarians and the touring All Blacks at Twickenham on 30 November 1974. It went without saying that New Zealand television would want to take it – live by satellite in the early hours of Sunday morning, their time. But who occupied the three places available in the commentary box for foreign language commentators – the Republic of Ireland, France and . . . Holland! And which three other countries took the whole of the match live, pictures and sound effects but no commentary, which they added themselves from their own television studios – Italy, Portugal and Turkey!

The surprising interest in televised rugby in countries where it would hardly be expected extends to the sale of telerecordings and films of the big matches by BBC Television Enterprises. Obviously such countries as France, New Zealand, Australia and Argentina and Japan (following their tours of Britain) are always in the market for the Internationals, either in full or in *Rugby Special* form, but one would not have thought that the following would be regular customers: US Air Force Colorado, Malaysia, Ghana, Singapore, Hong Kong, Kenya, the Netherlands, Taiwan, Thailand and Saudi Arabia.

Getting the Picture

I felt that the last named was the most surprising of all until it was explained to me by Guy Carr, head of BBC Television Enterprises, that the American Oil Company has its own television transmitter there to send out programmes to the many Americans employed in that part of the world and it seems they thoroughly enjoy sitting down in the evening to watch such things as the latest England–Wales match after their gruelling work at the oil drills.

BBC Television, which has a monopoly contract with the Four Home Unions to screen their Internationals, normally uses five cameras to cover the big matches at Twickenham. One is situated in front of the Royal Box in the West Stand on the half way line. Two more (one with a wide-angle lens and the other for 'tight' shots) are in a 'boat' between the upper and lower decks of the same stand. A fourth is on the South Terrace, to furnish a broad panorama of the Twickenham scene, to be used for head-on shots of kicks at goal at that end of the field and for little boys to jump up and make faces into the lens. The fifth camera is a portable one operated by a cameraman who sits with the band in the enclosure by the tunnel that leads out from the dressing-rooms under the Royal Box. His job is to pop up and take close-ups of the players emerging and shaking hands with the Queen if it is her day to be there, and also to take crowd shots from the field back into the West Stand during the course of the game and catch the reactions of the Royal Party, the Prime Minister or other dignitaries who may be present.

Bill Taylor, head of BBC rugby televising, masterminds the whole process and although he is at the ground he does not see anything of the game; not in the way the spectators do, that is. He is in the BBC's control vehicle parked behind the North Stand, sitting at the panel of five pictures coming from the cameras and deciding with the flick of a switch which picture will go out on the air at any given time.

In addition to those five cameras there are two more when the BBC, to give its Saturday afternoon *Grandstand* programme 'a sense of occasion', has Frank Bough there to introduce the whole show from Twickenham. A temporary studio is built on scaffolding high up in the corner between the North and West stands, with one camera inside for Bough to do his 'linking' and for interviews, and the other outside on the platform to pick up anything else that is happening.

All the cameras, in the tradition of anyone taking a photograph, have the sun behind them; that is they shoot almost exclusively from the West over towards the East Stand. But although one might think that Taylor prays for bright sunshine and therefore good pictures, that in fact is not the case.

Unrelenting sunshine from a clear blue sky is one of the big bugbears of televising matches at Twickenham. With the winter sun low in the sky the huge West Stand, 92 feet $10\frac{1}{2}$ inches high, casts a sharply defined shadow lengthwise down the middle of the field of play. Rugby being essentially a lateral game (the ball constantly moving back and forth in passing movements across-field from line-outs, scrums and rucks) the camera lens, unlike the human eye, is quite unable to strike a happy medium between the shaded part of the field and that in blazing sunshine. The result, as viewers well know, is gloom at the bottom of their screen and a burnt-out effect at the top. Do not adjust your set, nothing can be done about it – until some electronic genius comes up with some sort of compensating gadget that will overcome this problem. Meanwhile, on big match days at Twickenham, Bill Taylor and his colleagues can merely pray for just enough overcast to filter the sunshine and provide evenly diffused light.

In another 'boat' between the upper and lower decks of the West Stand is the television commentary position. By the mid-1970s, well-known voices such as those of Cliff Morgan and Peter West were no longer to be heard. From rugby commentating Cliff Morgan had first been given control of the BBC's sports broadcasts in general and then was promoted and placed in charge of 'outside broadcasts' of all types. Good for him, but a sad loss to rugby – his cheery personality on the air. Peter West stopped television commentating and only did radio when he took over from U. A. Titley the demanding job of rugby correspondent for *The Times*.

Now the undisputed dean of rugby commentary is Bill McLaren. The likable person he is comes across on the air and with his references to 'who-king' the ball back, 'phoot-up' in the scrum and 'pamming' the ball in line-outs leave no question whatsoever as to which side of the border he comes from. So familiar is he with the laws of rugby and so readily can he explain any tricky technicality that crops up during play that one almost feels that it was he who formulated them. But knowing what he is talking about is merely a reflection of the thoroughness with which he approaches his job. Diligently he attends the training sessions of teams which are going to feature in a match he will be covering so that when certain moves are made they come as no surprise to him (as they perhaps do to opponents) and he can quickly put viewers into the picture as to what precisely is happening. Before each game he prepares a huge chart on which are potted biographies and statistics of every player and all other persons connected with the event, plus a vast quantity of other succinctly listed information which can be brought into his commentary at any

This is the view for television commentators of today in their 'boat' between the upper and lower decks of the West Stand. Five television cameras in all cover the play.

appropriate time. These charts are masterpieces, in many and varied coloured inks, of capsuled background material. However, when the actual game gets under way he virtually never refers to it. It takes so much painstaking work to prepare it that everything is imprinted on his mind by the time the kick-off comes.

Rugby commentaries from Twickenham on the wireless in 1926 were among the first regular outside broadcasts transmitted by the BBC in those days of 'cat's whiskers' and crystal sets, and by the 1930s the first famous rugby voice of the air had emerged. Among other claims to fame of Teddy Wakelam, a great Harlequin man who was to write the history of the club, was that it was he who invented the idea of dividing the rugby field up into zones so as to make it easier for listeners to visualise precisely what was happening in a match. Each time an important game was broadcast the *Radio Times* would carry a plan of the playing area marked out into Zones A, B, C, D etc. and with this by his side the listener would follow Wakelam's commentary: '. . . a beautiful kick by Smith takes England from Zone B right up into G . . . from the scrum Scotland come back in attack, it goes out along the back line and Brown is brought down in Zone D . . .'

Although it may sound strange to modern ears, that was the way it was done right up until the war. After the war commentators felt that where play was could be quite accurately pinpointed by referring to the halfway line, the 10-yard line, the 25, or at such-and-such

The famous voice of Twickenham between the wars – Teddy Wakelam (right), pioneer rugby commentator. With him at the weird-looking microphones is a youthful John Snagge.

distance in from touch. But in the 1960s it was felt that the old system did have some merit and it was reintroduced. Its revival lasted for only two matches, however, and then it was dropped, through complaints from those who did have the *Radio Times* by their side and thought it unnecessarily complicated and from those who were not aware of the *Radio Times* key plan and wondered what was going on.

Although now naturally overshadowed by television, radio coverage still has a big audience. Just how big it is is impossible to gauge, since once you start sending things out on the radio waves (through the BBC's World Service as well as from the domestic transmitters) there is no precise way of checking just who is listening, from the hinterland of Kenya to the suburbs of Hong Kong, motorists on the M1 and men in ships.

When the All Blacks or one of the others are touring, the commentaries are of course beamed direct to the country concerned and there has been a tremendous improvement in reception since the Com-Pac (Commonwealth and Pacific) cable was opened, by the Queen, in 1963. Formerly the rugby broadcasts went across the world by shortwave radio link. Now the Com-Pac cable (which also carries phone calls and cablegrams) whisks them across the Atlantic to Canada, then by way of Honolulu and Fiji to Auckland. When New Zealand listeners, accustomed to the shortcomings of shortwave, heard their first commentaries on All Black matches in Britain by this system they wondered what on earth had happened. 'Sounds like the match is just up the road', they said happily.

As with the television commentaries at Twickenham, the radio commentators are in the 'boats' between the upper and lower decks of the West Stand. Alun Williams and Peter West are the ones who handle the main matches, shared, when it is a game against one of the major touring teams, by the radio man travelling with the side. British listeners will remember – who could ever forget? – the whizz-bang approach of New Zealand's Winston McCarthy, who was here first with the 'Kiwis' and then with Bob Stuart's side in 1953 and who brought a new dimension to what had formerly been an unemotional form of broadcasting. Bob Irvine, son of a famous All Black, W. R. ('Bull') Irvine of the 1924 Invincibles, is now the familiar voice whenever the New Zealanders are in Britain. The Springboks bring their own Afrikaans-speaking commentator and Afrikaans, with Welsh, Irish and French have always logically been the usual foreign tongues to be heard coming from the radio commentary positions at Twickenham.

But by 1975 we were on the verge of a multi-language explosion as far as radio coverage was concerned. With Fiji, Argentina, Japan and Tonga all undertaking visits in quick succession, and Rumania baying for admission, the regular British commentators at Twickenham were in for a wonderful variety of languages coming from the broadcasters at their side.

The visits by those minor rugby countries were what might be termed exploratory tours, so no live coverage went out to their home fans. The matches were covered from the BBC's World Service studios but when such tours become regular events Japan and the others will undoubtedly be sending their own radio commentators as the major tourists do. Ken Pragnell, as ardent a Harlequin man as Teddy Wakelam had been, is in charge of radio rugby coverage and I asked him what the Japanese commentary sounds like. 'Weird', he said. 'A great flow of unintelligible sounds and then words like "line-out" and "scrum" popping out at you all of a sudden. Just as with English being the common language for air pilots all over the world, they just do not bother to make up their own words for the technical terms in rugby when it goes into Japanese or into Spanish for the Argentinians, and so on.'

A NEW BREED OF PHOTOGRAPHERS

For a great number of years – from 1925 until the 1970s to be exact – the taking of photographs at Twickenham was a monopoly enjoyed by the Sport & General picture agency. As can so often be the case with a monopoly, this was not entirely satisfactory.

The feeling among rugby fans was that with no opposition to keep them on their toes the photographers on the sidelines at Twickenham had got very much into a rut. They seemed to be monotonously producing only four basic types of rugby pictures: line-outs, scrum-half sending the ball out to his backs, tries and place-kicks. This was not strictly true. Sport & General did occasionally come up with another type of action picture – a general shot of play, taken from up in the West Stand.

Perhaps in the old days this had been satisfactory enough but in the postwar era a new school of young rugby photographers grew up. Armed with all the new techniques of telephoto lenses and motorised cameras, they set out to bring much broader, more exciting photographic coverage to the game: midfield play (thanks to the telephoto lens), not just what happened along the touchline and the goal line; sequence shots (thanks to the motorised camera) of the build-up of a try right through to the touchdown, not merely the touchdown itself. But their activities were confined to the provinces. They could not reach the big matches at Twickenham because of the Sport &

Getting the Picture

General monopoly. However, in 1971, something happened which, if it was not too good for the picture agency concerned, was great for the new breed of photographers. Sport & General got into financial difficulties and the Rugby Union had no option but to throw Twickenham open to competitive photography.

Sport & General used to cover each match with four photographers and sometimes a fifth up in the West Stand. Now nine men are allowed on the fringes of the ground and four more in the stand, the tickets being allocated to the newspapers on a rota basis. They would like more but the Rugby Union's limitation of nine on the field is a strict one, based on the fact that there is not a great deal of space between the touchlines and the ringside seats and hordes of photographers could make for dangerous collisions with players and touch-judges.

To rush the pictures to Fleet Street there are a batch of messengers clustered under the clock at the southern end of the East Stand. After twenty-five minutes' play photographers dash across with their exposed film to the messengers, who then head off at speed into town. They can do the trip from Twickenham to their offices in half an hour; within ten minutes of the films arriving at the studio finished prints are ready. The reason for this particular operation is to catch the out-of-town editions of the Sunday papers, which go to press at around four-thirty on Saturday afternoon. So if any International player wants to be assured of good national picture coverage on Sunday for a spectacular try he is well advised to score it within the first twenty-five minutes of the match.

The photographers, of course, continue taking shots throughout the whole game but later events merely make the London editions of the Sundays, and naturally the Monday papers.

Just as in soccer, where goals scored are the essential subjects to photograph, in rugby it is the tries that count with picture editors. But it stands to reason that if a team makes a move that catches their opponents napping and it results in a try, the photographers are likely to be caught napping too. Not every International try at Twickenham has been recorded for posterity. As one veteran agency photographer said to me: 'I'd like to have a pound for every try we've missed.'

Among those not to be found in the photographic files are several of the most momentous in the history of the game.

In the England-Wales match of 1923 Wakefield kicked off high upfield into a howling gale. The ball ballooned back into the arms of Leo Price (Oxford and Harlequins, England hockey as well as rugby cap) and he decided to essay a drop kick at goal. Like the kick-off, however, it was blown back, again into his arms. The Welshmen, as is usual when anybody tries a drop at goal, turned to see how he had made out. They were taken quite unawares. He sailed past them and scored under the posts, a try which not only created a record for the quickest opening try in Test rugby (14 seconds) but also was that rare if not unique occurrence of a try being scored from the kick-off without the opposition touching the ball. Needless to say the photographers who in those days patrolled the touchlines in long overcoats with their Micropress 4×5 plate cameras were as much taken by surprise as were the Welsh.

In England's match against France in 1924 the spectacular three-quarter H. C. ('Catchy') Catchside, of Percy Park, scored a sensational try when he broke clear and, confronted by the crouching French full-back, did a high jump over him to get to the line – which would have made one of the best rugby pictures of that or any other year.

No still photographer was in position to get a shot of Obolensky scoring his famous second try against New Zealand in 1936.

Andy Hancock touched down after his incredible 95-yard run against Scotland in 1965 without a photographer being anywhere near him. When Hancock had set off on that run, Scotland had been pressing and everybody – including the photographers – had expected another score from them. With cameras at the ready all the photographers were clustered around the England goal line, and when Hancock took off in the direction of the other end of the field it was a certainty that if none of the Scottish players could keep up with him, no photographer could.

Unexpectedness was of course the reason the photographers missed the Hancock try and other great ones at Twickenham but in the old days – up till the early 1960s in fact – the newsreel cameramen were in action at the ground and fortunately it was possible to take 'frames' from their movie sequences. Thus it was that the great Obolensky effort did not go unrecorded and the series of pictures of the try from film clips are now familiar to all rugby fans. Likewise Peter Jackson's match-winner against Australia in injury time in 1958 and Richard Sharp's, with three devastating dummies, against Scotland in 1963. But by the time Andy Hancock came along television had put the newsreels out of business. A pity, since getting still pictures from television coverage is at present unsatisfactory. Although it sounds somewhat primitive the only way it is possible is to set up a camera in front of the television screen and take fuzzy photographs as the television recording is re-run.

Chapter 16

When the War Was Over

In contrast to the First World War, when Twickenham was merely used for grazing horses, during the Second the ground took very much of a hammering, not so much from enemy action but from occupation by other than rugby fans. The whole property was requisitioned for a variety of uses. The extensive iron railings around the East Car Park were removed for scrap and that area split up into allotments. The offices and dressing-rooms in the West Stand, and the restaurants, were occupied by Civil Defence units and every bit of open space under the stands was used for storage and for garaging army trucks and fire-fighting appliances. Anyone driving past the West Car Park with happy memories of pre-match picnic lunches there must have wondered if those days would ever return. It had become a gigantic coal dump.

Fortunately the ground escaped any direct hits, but on 1 July 1944, when a V-Bomb landed on nearby Talma Gardens, the West Stand was damaged, and the roofs of all three stands were constantly having gaps put through them by ack-ack shell splinters. There were no complaints from the Rugby Union because of course it had its contribution to make to the war effort along with everybody else, but as all who came under requisition were to learn full well wartime occupants are no respecters of property and when Twickenham was formally de-requisitioned on 30 September 1945 it was in a fine old mess. Apart from such things as the holes in the roofs, which had been left unrepaired since the rain merely dripped down on to the upper decks of the stands and not into the offices and storage space below, there had been no regular care and maintenance for six years and immediate efforts had to be made to get the place into some sort of order for the first two big matches of the 1945–6 season – an England XV versus the New Zealand Army Kiwis on 24 November and the resumption of the Varsity Match on 12 December.

For some time portions of the stands could not be used, particularly the upper West, which was decidedly damp in wet weather and

The 1950s were enlivened by Marques (with ball) and Currie (left), perhaps the best pair of locks England have ever had. This (unassisted) leap by Marques shows why he had the reputation of being one of rugby's greatest line-out jumpers.

When the War Was Over

dangerous in high winds, but in January 1946 it was possible to get a licence from the Ministry of Works for the expenditure of £3,336 for essential work. The Rugby Union's claim for £12,000 compensation for the results of requisition was settled at a compromise of £7,000, and a tremendous amount of work by the Twickenham staff on repairs, cleaning and painting had the ground returning to something like normality when the Internationals were resumed again in the 1946-7 season.

If anyone had hoped for a repetition after the Second World War of the golden era English rugby had enjoyed after the First, they were sorely disappointed. Unlike the 1920s, when Wakefield set Twickenham alight with his inspired leadership of a consistently winning England side, no one emerged in the last postwar era. Ireland, which had been neutral during the war, had their great and only period of dominance of the International Championship. They were probably fitter than their war-weary opponents.

By 1953, however, England had entered a sequence lasting to 1963 in which they wound up at the top of the Championship table with something approaching the regularity of the glorious Wakefield days. In those eleven years they won the Championship four times and shared it twice, which, considering the fact that since then they have never topped the list, was at least a sort of rolled-golden era.

Twickenham fans remember Nim Hall as their first real star of the immediate postwar era. He was capped in the first of the resumed Internationals in 1947, finished with seventeen appearances, thirteen of them as England's captain. The fact that he played either at fly-half, centre or full-back was both a reflection of his versatility and of the paucity of good players at that time. There was strength up front – such solid forwards like Eric Evans and Albert Agar, both later to be England selectors. Evans was capped thirty times, just one short of Wakefield's record, and was still an International at the age of thirty-seven.

In the latter part of the 1950s England was better served as far as backs were concerned and this was one of the main reasons for the successful showing of the team. Ted Woodward was a great favourite with the crowds at Twickenham – the burly butcher on the wing who was a firm believer in running through, not round, opponents. Jeeps came on the scene in 1956 and Peter Jackson in the same year – two of England's greatest ever at scrum-half and wing, with Butterfield and Davies in the centre, again among the best combinations England has ever produced in that part of the field. It would seem that 1956 was a vintage year, for it saw the debuts also of four of England's most

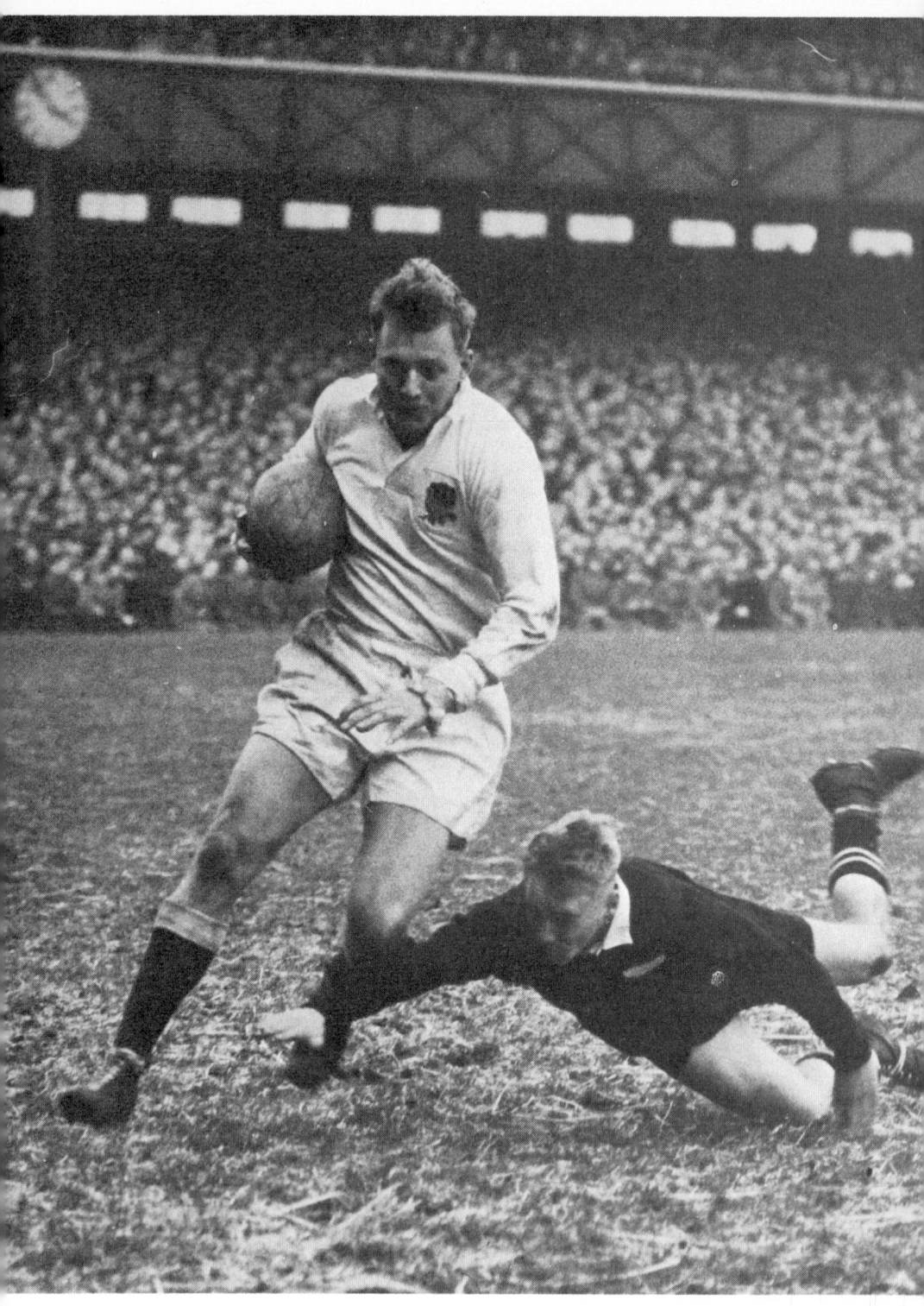

Ted Woodward, the burly butcher, seen here eluding D. D. Wilson of New Zealand, was a great Twickenham favourite on the wing in the course of his fifteen caps 1952–6.

memorable forwards – Ron Jacobs, Peter Robbins and that magnificent pair of locks and line-out jumpers, Marques and Currie.

Most of these carried on into the 1960s, to be joined by three outstanding newcomers. 'Budge' Rogers, that great loose forward, became the one who was at last to beat Wakefield's record for England appearances and earned himself an OBE for it. Richard Sharp burst forth on the Twickenham public in 1960, as a last-minute replacement for flu-struck Bev Risman in the match against Wales, and his slicing through the Welsh defenders that day was perhaps the most spectacular debut the ground has ever seen. England supporters are everlastingly grateful to him, for now they do not have to remain silent when Irish and Welsh fans go on and on about Jackie Kyle and Cliff Morgan. The other new star emerged in the 1960s. After the regular full-back, Don Rutherford, dropped out of International rugby in 1967, later to become one of the two Assistant Secretaries of the RFU, his place was taken by one of the most colourful, not to say controversial, players England has produced in the postwar era – Bob Hiller.

Chapter 17

The Notorious Match

A Twickenham International of the 1950s which stays vividly in the mind – not only of those present but also of the millions who saw it on television who were spared none of the gory details – was a strange mixture of the good and bad in rugby.

PETER JACKSON FRUSTRATES THE AUSSIES
England v. Australia, 1 February 1958

This, the dirtiest International ever played at Twickenham, would best have been forgotten had it not been for one of the most exciting match-winning tries ever seen at the ground.

The teams:

England: J. G. G. Hetherington (Northampton); P. B. Jackson (Coventry), J. Butterfield (Northampton), M. S. Phillips (Oxford), P. H. Thompson (Headingly); J. P. Horrocks-Taylor (Cambridge), R. E. G. Jeeps (Northampton); C. R. Jacobs (Northampton), E. Evans (Sale, capt.), G. W. Hastings (Gloucester), R. W. D. Marques (Cambridge), J. D. Currie (Oxford), P. G. D. Robbins (Oxford), A. Ashcroft (Waterloo), R. E. Syrett (Wasps).

Australia: T. G. Curley; R. Phelps, J. Lenehan, K. J. Donald, S. W. White; A. Simmons, D. M. Connor; R. A. L. Davidson (capt.), J. V. Brown, G. N. Vaughan, D. Emanuel, A. R. Millar, N. M. Hughes, K. J. Ryan, P. Fenwicke.

Referee: R. C. Williams (Ireland).

It was not a good Wallaby touring side. From the outset things went wrong. They won only two of their first six matches. No major touring team had ever suffered the ignominy of losing more matches than they won but when things were tallied up at the end of the tour it was found that the 1957–8 Australians had come very close to it.

The Notorious Match

They did in fact fail to win more matches than they won, with their three draws and sixteen defeats outnumbering their seventeen victories. One reason was that the selectors had included more young, untried players than is usual on such tours, since they took the long-term view that it would be good for the future of the game in Australia for them to come home having been blooded in big-time rugby. Unfortunately, without a depth of experience down through the team, they proved unable to cope with any team they met which had some measure of strength.

Under the circumstances nobody derided them for their lack of success. But what the British crowds were unhappy about was that, perhaps through frustration, they turned to playing some of the roughest football ever consistently displayed by any touring team.

England were Champions at the time, having become so in the previous season with their first Grand Slam since 1928, and when the Australians took the field against them at Twickenham the tourists seemed determined to achieve a victory that would more than compensate for failures elsewhere. And their determination was expressed physically. In the first half one England player had to be assisted from the field and was unable to return. Another was being carried off on a stretcher but resumed playing when he made the quick decision to jump off and take up his position again. Three England players finished the match in such a state of concussion that they did not really know what was going on.

The Twickenham crowd is a traditionally quiet one compared to those of other International grounds as regards voicing either approval or disapproval. But this day the reaction to what was happening on the field was not only the most violent ever heard at Twickenham. Rarely has such sustained booing, hooting and screaming been directed against a team at any other International venue. Their animosity towards the Australians went right out of control, but it must be said that it is difficult to maintain a reputation for not being particularly demonstrative when continued fouls in the field of play culminate in someone running over deliberately to kick a home player lying on the ground after being tackled into touch.

The aggression started right from the kick-off, with the referee, Williams, blowing hard for penalties, at least two of which were within kicking range. However, England's full-back John Hetherington, playing in his first International and perhaps wondering what he had got himself into, could not settle down sufficiently to turn them into goals. England attacked through the barrage of late tackles and obstruction. Horrocks-Taylor shaved the wrong side of a post with a drop-kick. Peter Jackson, who was to be the hero of the day, made two great runs down the right touchline with his typically deceptive stop-go technique before being brought down short each time.

Ten minutes before the interval Australia had reduced the opposition to fourteen players when Horrocks-Taylor was helped off, dragging a leg immobilised by a kicked calf muscle. Ashcroft was taken out of the scrum to play at centre and Butterfield, visibly groggy from some hard tackles directed towards him as the world-class key man in the England back line, moved to fly-half. Inspired by the numerical advantage they had achieved, the Wallabies pressed and Lenehan, kicker of wobbly penalties but not as amusingly as Scotland's P. C. Brown, managed to get one over the crossbar. Half-time: England 0, Australia 3.

During the break Eric Evans decided that his side were missing the power of Ashcroft in the line-outs, so he brought him back into the pack and moved the mobile Peter Robbins out into the centre. It was a good bit of thinking because the backline functioned much more smoothly now as England went all-out on attack to offset their one-man shortage.

From a scrum just outside the Australian 25 Jeeps whipped the ball out to Butterfield, who made some ground before transferring to Phillips, who beat Wallaby full-back Curley to the corner. England 3, Australia 3.

This did not find favour with the Australians, who vented their spleen on the winger, Peter Thompson. He was laid out by a crushing tackle by three of the tourists and no sooner had he recovered from this than he was the victim of a vicious kick by Lenehan while lying on the ground after being forced into touch.

Butterfield was the next to feel their wrath. Late-tackled after he had passed, he was seen to be writhing on the ground for several minutes. The crowd were incensed and Twickenham rang with their booing as he was being carried off on a stretcher. He then made his miraculous recovery, but was in truth in no fit state to continue. This sort of thing was liable to happen all too frequently in International rugby before the sensible introduction of substitutes.

In the highly charged atmosphere (many in the stands were now on their feet almost constantly, cheering England on and booing the Australians), the game went on. Under pressure, Jeeps miscued a relieving kick and Curley, going at top speed, brilliantly scooped up the ball as it bounced near touch, steadied himself and sent over a superb angled drop kick. England 3, Australia 6.

Five minutes later, just as full time was coming up, England were awarded a penalty thirty yards out and the ball was given to Hetherington. As he made his preparations for the kick he was obviously shaky

Two of the men who helped to make England one of the strongest sides in the International Championship in the 1950s – Dickie Jeeps and Peter Jackson, about to cope with R. Phelps in the England–Australia match in 1958.

and afterwards it transpired that he along with Thompson and Butterfield had played out the majority of the second half in a state of concussion. He rose to the occasion now, however, even though the ball only just scraped over the crossbar.

England 6, Australia 6; and it was felt that with the final whistle about to go at least justice had been done; the high proportion of Sydney toughs in the touring team had been shown that intimidation does not win matches against men resolute enough to stand up to it.

But the final whistle was not about to go. A measure of just how much time had been taken up by injuries was the fact that extra time went on and on – to five minutes, ten minutes and still the referee showed no sign of bringing the game to a close. Although nobody was in a jocular mood it might have been felt that as the well-known Twickenham evening mist began to settle this match would prove unique in being the first International in which bad light had stopped play.

Then in the gloom out came the ball along the England backline to Peter Jackson on the right wing. He received from Malcolm Phillips thirty yards out. Phelps, who had resolutely marked Jackson throughout the game, came at him and Jackson made to fend him off. 'I didn't actually hand him off', Jackson said afterwards. 'I withdrew my hand at the last moment, throwing him off balance sufficiently for me to elude him.'

With only Curley, the full-back, between him and the line he did one of the famous Jackson hesitations, placing Curley in a quandary as to whether he was going to try to go inside him or outside him. 'My natural instinct was to side-step inside,' said Jackson. 'Fortunately he broadcast his intention of anticipating this move and consequently I went the other way.' But no sooner had he left Curley floundering than he realised his momentary loss of pace had allowed Phelps time to get up into position for another go at him. This time his Aussie marker made no mistake, tackling him firmly and correctly – towards touch. And Jackson provided an object lesson for any aspiring wing three-quarter. He took the tackle with his inside shoulder down, all his weight veering away from touch as he dived over to ground the ball inches away from the corner flag.

The applause was thunderous and continued that way as Jackson walked back to take up his position again, for unbelievably, even despite the time taken for Hetherington's unsuccessful conversion attempt, the game was still not over. Any soccer fan, used to the kissing antics of that other game, must have been bewildered at how Jackson's colleagues virtually ignored him and the man himself was seen not even to raise a smile. 'After the game,' he said, 'one spectator came up to me and said, "By golly, after scoring a try like that you walked back looking downright mournful. If I had scored the try I would have jumped for joy." I hadn't the heart to tell him I felt like death warmed up.'

And when eventually, at 9–6 to England, the last whistle did shrill out, Jackson had thus frustrated the Australians with one of the greatest match-winning tries ever seen at Twickenham in the longest International ever played.

Chapter 18

'Anyone Got a Spare Ticket?'

The takings for the 18,000 at the first International at Twickenham in 1910 were £2,250. By 1975 this figure had risen to £100,000-plus for a capacity house and it was in this year that for the first time different prices were charged depending on the position of seats in the stands.

Oddly enough there had never been any serious complaints about the fact that for the Internationals you paid a flat rate for a stand ticket at Twickenham no matter where your seat was. Two reasons for this were that in the first place, the demand being so great, one was only too glad to get a ticket anywhere, and secondly it has always been said that 'there is no really bad seat at Twickenham'. Proof of this is that some years ago the Rugby Union felt a bit self-conscious about charging the same price for a seat behind a pillar as for an unrestricted view on the half way line. Not that there are actually any seats that are slap-bang behind a pillar, the construction of the stands being such that gangways and exits invariably coincide with the position of the obstructions. Nevertheless it was felt that some seats were not of the best, so 200 were withdrawn from sale in the normal way, being classified as seats which could be bought 'with an offer to view'. In other words, would-be purchasers could come to the ground beforehand, see precisely where their seat was and then decide whether or not to buy. Which is exactly what they did and when the Rugby Union soon found that all these so-called bad seats were always snapped up they felt that it was no longer necessary to make this dispensation.

It might have been thought that those in the North Stand, viewing the pitch from one end, were not getting as good a deal for the same amount of money as those watching at the side from the middle of the field but it is interesting to note that Adrian Stoop, when he retired from active play and became an RFU administrator, liked to watch from the North Stand rather than from the plum seats in the committee box. 'I like the head-on view', he always used to say.

Willie John McBride, leader of the triumphant Irish against England in 1972 and in a couple of years' time to become leader of the magnificent Lions in South Africa.

The system of an over-all rate for stand seats (£1 in the 1950s, £1 10s in the 1960s and £2 in the early 1970s) was abandoned in 1975 when another increase had to be made to keep up with inflation, and the feeling of the Rugby Union was that with the cost now becoming unavoidably high it was only right that the tickets should be graded in price as has always been the case with theatres and other forms of entertainment.

So, as a matter of interest to the readers of this book in years to come, when the price of tickets will undoubtedly have gone up still further, these were the newly established rates for the Internationals at Twickenham in the 1974–5 season:

West and East Stands: upper and lower, centre	£3.50
West and East Stands: upper and lower, wings	2.50
North Stand	2.00
West and East Ringside, centre	1.50
West and East Ringside, wings	1.25
Enclosures	0.75
Ground	0.60

The first all-ticket match was England v. Wales in 1953. The ticket application forms from the clubs are on bright yellow sheets, somewhat bigger than foolscap, on which are printed the various categories from the most expensive down to ground tickets and each club fills in the number required of each type, totals up the cost and sends a cheque for the full amount along with the application. When once I visited the ticket office I watched these being checked and noticed on the top of one pile the application from Northampton – £1,358.70 worth of tickets! I mentioned to the young man at work on that stack that it seemed quite a whopping figure. 'Not exceptional', he said. 'You'll see others over on that other desk for £3,000 and more. And of course when England are playing Wales at Twickenham, the application from London Welsh . . .' He merely raised his eyebrows and grinned and left it at that.

The deadline for ticket applications is 15 October for the two regular Internationals at Twickenham which take place in the early months of the following year and since they are always oversubscribed they can be said to be sold out on that date. Each season, more than £100,000 has to be returned to the disappointed. The Rugby Union is scrupulously fair. Each application is given a number when it arrives and throughout its life in the ticket office it is always referred to by that number, never by the name of the club that has sent it in. This means that when the 'scaling down' is done (when it is decided what proportion of each club's application they will receive) there is no likelihood of any one club being specially favoured. The little Puddletown Rugby Football Club gets precisely the same percentage of their small application as mighty Harlequins get of their big one.

In the weeks prior to an International the telephone in the ticket office never stops ringing and people who phone in trying to get tickets all have to be told the same thing: 'Sorry, no tickets are sold to the general public.' A small percentage of ground tickets do go on sale at Alfred Hays Ltd, the ticket agency at the top of Whitehall and at their branches, but what the people who phone in are really after, grandstand seats, are allocated only to committee members, who certainly deserve them in view of the tremendous amount of work they do for the game without payment of any sort, and to clubs (including, of course, the universities, the Services and schools), who are the ones who play and support rugby week after week. Often those who phone in for tickets will not take no for an answer and the most popular form

Hiller, quite unable to stop Barry John getting his kick away in the 1972 England–Wales International. Welsh centre Bergiers is on the left and Peter Dixon right.

of special pleading is, of course, the well-worn cliché: 'I'm just back from abroad, I haven't seen an International for eight (ten? twelve?) years and I'm just dying to see one again . . .'

Players taking part in an International each get six complimentary tickets. Each visiting Union is allocated 900 tickets to sell to their own supporters, which does not sound like a great number but England get even fewer when they go to Cardiff Arms Park, Murrayfield or Lansdowne Road, since those grounds have nothing like the same amount of seated accommodation as Twickenham.

Walkers of Twickenham have been printing the tickets for the ground since it opened and now, what with all these additional matches with Fiji and Tonga and other new touring countries, the print order for tickets each season amounts to 280,000. Bearing this in mind, plus the fact that they have been at it for more than sixty years, it is a wonderful tribute to the girls who check the tickets before they leave the printing shop and those who check them again when they reach the ticket office that there has never been a 'double'. Nobody has ever arrived at Twickenham to find somebody else in his seat; or even worse (it has never happened), to find that your ticket for 'Entrance C, Row 14, Seat 1006', is valueless because there is no such seat, and if there were you would have been sitting somewhere half way down the Whitton Road.

When George Young, who is in charge of the ticket operation and the 50 turnstiles and 120 gatesmen for a big match, went to work at Twickenham in 1946 the ticket office was very much a hole-in-the-wall affair in the not particularly spacious accommodation for the RFU staff up the stairs under the West Stand. But when the New Zealand Army Kiwis came on tour to invigorate the game again and the first batch of postwar stars began to emerge – England's Nim Hall, Kendall-Carpenter and Eric Evans, Ireland's Jackie Kyle and Karl Mullen, France's Jean Prat, Scotland's Kininmonth, Ken Jones and Cliff Morgan of Wales – the demand for tickets was such that more and more space was needed, until by the end of the 1960s there was nothing for it but to move the ticket office out and give it a building of its own. This is now just inside the Rowland Hill Gates.

The activities of the ticket touts outside the ground constitute something which the Rugby Union has come to find that nothing much can be done about. The committee did once undertake a thorough investigation of the matter, from which they learned that the spivs who do the selling are not the ones who get hold of the tickets, apart from the odd spare picked up from a spectator on his way to the match. The whole operation is masterminded up in London by the big boys who also do Wembley and the other sports venues where

Defenders in disarray as Earle Kirton scores in the All Blacks' runaway victory over England in 1967, supported by Lochore, Tremain and Birtwhistle.

ticket demand outstrips supply. The Rugby Union has now of necessity become philosophical about the fact that when 70,000 tickets are sent out for a match there is bound to be a certain amount of 'spillage' that gets into the hands of the spivs.

'GET YOUR PROGRAMMES!'

The first ever 'souvenir programme' for an International at Twickenham was for England's match against the Fourth Springboks on 5 January 1952. Previous to that, the programme was a rather mean-looking thing consisting merely of a folded-over card with an aerial picture of the ground on the front and inside the line-up of the two teams. It was thanks to Chris Lampard that we got the well produced brochure that we know today.

'Anyone Got a Spare Ticket?'

Lampard had been a Lieut.-Commander RN in destroyers during the war and after he was demobbed he was having a drink one day with his friend Morris Murdoch, also an ex-destroyer man, and he said to him: 'Well, what do we do now?' Murdoch had been a director of a printing firm, Welbecson Press, and when he said he proposed to continue in this field Lampard evolved with him the idea of producing souvenir programmes for anyone likely to favour the notion. They formed a company, Programme Publications Ltd, and in 1947 Jack Solomons was the first to embrace the idea for his big fight promotions. Bertram Mills' circus was next and they were quickly followed by Wimbledon, the British Open, the Horse of the Year Show, the Varsity Boat Race. Lampard turned to football, and Chelsea was the first to have its own illustrated programme, followed by Arsenal, although today these clubs have themselves taken over the involved work of producing these programmes each week of the lengthy soccer season.

When the cheery, gregarious Lampard approached the Rugby Football Union the conservative element which used to exert considerable influence on Twickenham decisions were unenthusiastic. But in 1951 Lampard was able to get permission to publish as a trial run a souvenir programme for that December's Varsity match. The novelty was such a success that for the first International of the season a month later the experiment was repeated, to become henceforth a regular part of the Twickenham scene for all big matches.

Not unnaturally the gentlemen of the spiv world were quick to realise that Lampard was on to a good thing. They started producing, for sale outside the ground, programmes which outwardly bore a resemblance to the official product. Not only were these quite unofficial, not being a 'concession' granted by the RFU for a percentage of the purchase price as with Programme Publications Ltd, but also anyone foolish enough to buy a copy soon found that it was what is called today a rip-off. The team line-ups were not accurate and the rest of the contents sparse.

Nowadays Twickenham fans are wise to this and the publishers of unofficial programmes have a pretty thin time of it, but for some years the wide boys were a thorn in the side of the producers of the official programme, since in law there is no way of stopping people from exploiting the fact that there is a mug born every minute. Lampard had no recourse but to have loudspeaker vans patrolling the approaches to Twickenham and outside the station, exhorting the crowds not to buy a programme until they could get the official ones inside the ground. It was especially necessary to think of fans coming from far afield. So, when France were visiting, the announcements went out in French and on Calcutta Cup days Lampard saw to it that Scots

Roger Uttley, a hero of the 1974 Lions as a loose forward and a mainstay of England's pack as a lock.

were made to feel at home, with a voice coming from the loudspeakers: 'Ach, mon, you'll no be buying a programme the noo, you'll be waiting until you get into the groond.'

For Twickenham's biggest drawcard, the England–Wales clash, 52,000 programmes are printed and proportionally fewer for the other Internationals. They are always sold out but not all of them at the ground. A percentage are held back at the offices of Programme Publications in Battersea for postal sales, a thriving section of the operation. Requests for copies come by mail from all over the world. For example there is a gentleman in Japan, a Japanese not a homesick Englishman, who has now put in a standing order for every rugby programme they print, which includes the Cardiff Arms Park programmes, since the firm caters for all the Welsh home Internationals as well.

As a group the Welsh are the greatest programme collectors of them all. At the beginning of each season letters pour in 'from the valleys', as Lampard puts it, for advance copies not only for all their own Internationals but also England's. Individually, those who would qualify for the Guinness Book of Records as the compulsive buyers of programmes are: P. D. E. Gibbs of Upper Richmond Road, London SW15, R. A. Drinkwater of Acton, and 812 Corporal Jago of Calmouth, Cornwall, who have bought anything from one to three copies of every programme published from the start in 1951. One can be sure that they are in touch also with Murrayfield, Lansdowne Road and other sources of programmes around the world, so that their shelves must be pleasantly weighed down by rugby nostalgia.

The programmes at Twickenham were originally a shilling each and crept up through inflation to 1s 6d, to 10p and, in 1975, to 15p. Every big match day there are no fewer than sixty programme sellers. For some years those who wrote the articles in the programmes were paid 25 guineas a time but this was likely to be boosted to keep up with inflation. Advertisers – of cigarettes (the ideal thing to keep rugby players match fit), after-shave lotion (to cover up the smell of embrocation when taking girl friend out after the match), banking facilities, rugby gear, rugby book publications, jockstraps etc. – pay at the rate of £90 per page.

The programmes are produced by an editorial staff of five and their big headache, of course, is getting the teams right. The middle eight pages, which contain the team line-ups and the thumbnail photos and potted biographies of the players, do not go to press until the very last moment. This is not only to allow for changes – Risman comes down with flu on the Friday and Sharp is picked to take his place – but because the publishers can have difficulty in getting in good time the chosen team for a match, let alone changes. This applies mainly to the big touring sides, who often put off making their final selection for an International until they can be sure of match fitness of key players. What Chris Lampard does on such occasions is to take it upon himself to pick the All Blacks, Wallabies or Springboks team and go ahead hoping that it will not be necessary to make many adjustments when the presses start to roll.

The biggest headache they ever had in this regard was when the 1969–70 Springboks were on their notorious 'demo tour'. Of necessity that team went into hiding between matches to avoid being pestered. This meant that the programme compilers had to track down the tourists and then, with cloak-and-dagger phone calls in the middle of the night, get their team selections from them. So well kept was the secret of where they were before the opening match against Oxford University at Twickenham (they were at the secluded Dormy Hotel outside Bournemouth), that any hope of a printed programme was abandoned and all that the spectators got was a list of the teams on a mimeographed sheet of foolscap.

Later in that tour when the England v. South Africa match was coming up at Twickenham on 20 December 1969, Lampard decided that all that could be done was for him to choose the Springbok side and trust to luck. He did, however, manage to get hold of the South Africans' manager just before they went to press and he read the team out to him over the phone. 'Splendid', said the manager. 'But do you mind if we make one change? We'd like to play Van Der Watt on the left wing instead of Gert Muller.'

The programme for the England–Ireland match at Twickenham on 14 February 1970 is unique in that the leading article was by a player taking part in the game, seemingly a flagrant violation of rugby's strict laws on professionalism. But how this came about was not without its amusing side. The left wing position in the Ireland team, as printed in the programme, was occupied by W. J. Brown, of Malone, but at the last minute he had to drop out. To everybody's surprise, not to mention that of the man himself, the selectors called up Tony O'Reilly, who was not even in the printed list of Irish reserves. He had retired from the International scene as long ago as 1963 but had recently been having a few club games, not with a view to a comeback but to ward off what looked like a middle-age spread developing at his office desk as an executive of importance. So unexpected was his recall that it was said that on the Saturday previous to the match he had been in the London Irish clubhouse inquiring whether anyone could get him a couple of tickets for the game. Summoned to join the Irish party, he set up some sort of first by arriving for the training

During the England–Wales match of 1974 a characteristic switch of direction by Phil Bennett has him apparently taking on team-mates Mervyn Davies (8), Gareth Edwards (9) and Shaw (1).

session just prior to the match in a chauffeur-driven Rolls-Royce.

In the game itself O'Reilly got little to do but throw the ball in at line-outs, not one useful pass coming his way throughout the proceedings. All he really got out of that – to the Irish – notorious match in which Bob Hiller beat them with two devastating drop kicks, was concussion. So against the run of the play was England's 9–3 win that O'Reilly in his concussed state left the field, as the teams filed off, happily under the impression that Ireland had recorded a splendid victory.

However, there were no repercussions from his apparently terrible crime against amateur status. He had waived payment for the article, so the true spirit of the game had not been sullied.

Chapter 19

The Marathon Try

If one attempts to assess the great tries by individual players, in an effort to arrive at which was the greatest, how can one really gauge whether this one was better than that one? There are so many different yardsticks to apply.

A player may run fifty yards on his own to score but with his team already well ahead on points is it therefore a less good try than that by another player who does precisely the same thing but whose effort is the match-winner? A player may make a break sixty yards out and by sheer speed outdistance all the defenders – is that a better try than the man who runs in from merely thirty yards but in the course of it brilliantly eludes four would-be tacklers in succession?

Some great Twickenham try scorers readily come to mind: H. L. Price, who scored from the kick-off against Wales in 1923 before any of the opposition had touched the ball; Obolensky's famous diagonal run against New Zealand in 1935; London Counties winger Chris Winn outfoxing the Springboks in 1951 by following up an unsuccessful long-range shot at goal so quickly that he beat the men behind the line to the touchdown; Peter Jackson's injury time match-winner against Australia in 1958; Sharp's against Scotland in 1963 following three devastating dummies which beat in turn the breakaways, the centres and the full-back; Ireland's Mike Flynn stealing the match from England in 1972 with a breakthrough on the call of time.

They were all so different that it is difficult to decide which was the greatest, but we do know by actual measurement which was the longest run-in for a try at Twickenham – or at any other International ground, for that matter.

HANCOCK'S TRY
England v. Scotland, 20 March 1965

There were two indications of what a bolt-from-the-blue surprise Andy Hancock's try was in the 1965 Calcutta Cup match. The first is that although you can go to a picture agency and get a photo of any of the important tries scored at Twickenham in recent years you will not find one of the Hancock effort. The reason was simple. With the final whistle coming up Scotland were leading 3–0 and maintaining sustained pressure on the England line, with every sign that they would augment their score. So all the photographers had congregated at that end to record the event, with the result that when Hancock made his 95-yard dash there were no photographers at the other goal line to get a shot of him touching down. And the other thing was that a Scottish rugby writer in the press box was so certain, along with everybody else, that it was a Scottish victory that he had written his stirring piece about Scotland's first victory at Twickenham since 1938 – after more than a quarter of a century the Scots had laid the Twickenham bogey! – and he had the copy in his hand ready to dash to the phone and catch his paper's early editions. So that when Hancock sensationally brought the scores level and Twickenham exploded with joyous cheers, he had to do a frenzied rewrite.

The match itself is not really worth recalling in detail. Had it not been for the Hancock try it would merely have been classified as one of the drab ones in the Calcutta Cup series and forgotten.

There had been incessant rain throughout the morning and early afternoon, to the extent of one correspondent writing that 'only with great ingenuity had the picnic parties in the car park managed to keep the smoked salmon sandwiches dry'. The rain stopped just before kick-off and it remained clear but the ground was so waterlogged that any advantage was to traditional Scottish forward play, in the hands or rather at the feet of such as Rollo, Campbell-Lamerton and Stagg. From the interminable line-outs and scrums the ball rarely progressed beyond the Scottish halves Hastie and Chisholm and the England pair, S. J. S. Clarke and Mike Weston, the fondness for kicking of the last-named being for once justified under the conditions. Up to his last-minute receipt of the ball Hancock on the left wing had received only two passes all day, both of which he dropped.

Chisholm potted a goal just after the start of the second half and as the match slushed towards its close a Scottish win seemed a fair enough decision in the circumstances. But the radical change in the scoreline came as the referee was looking at his watch.

England were pinned in their 25 when the soapy ball slithered out to D. J. Whyte on the Scottish right wing. He seemed to see the chance for a try by running infield. A maul formed when he ran into trouble and the ball came back to Weston. Under pressure, fifteen yards from the England line, it would have been logical for him to have booted it into touch. Instead he passed it to the only uncommitted Englishman

The Marathon Try

in the vicinity – Hancock. In view of Whyte's inland excursion Hancock was confronted with a vacant touchline, so he started running.

He went perilously close to going into touch when he swerved to avoid the Scottish flanker Grant diving across at him just after he passed the 25. So he moved infield to give himself more space to manoeuvre as he was coming up to halfway and he could see Stewart Wilson, the full-back, ahead of him, waiting just inside his own half. He decided to take the outside course around him if he could avoid the tackle, which in fact he did, Wilson not getting a good take-off on the wet turf as he launched himself.

Hancock recalled afterwards that he had the well-known thundering hooves behind him as he carried on towards what was now the open Scottish line but he dared not look around to see whether it was support or would-be tacklers who were the front-runners in his wake for fear of losing vital pace in the heavy going. As it was he felt that his 'feet were in glue – my calves ached and my lungs felt as though they were bursting'.

On the Scottish 25 he was conscious of a blue shirt coming at him from mid-field (it turned out to be Laughland, one of the centres) and for the final twenty yards he just forced himself on, to the accompaniment of Laughland pounding away behind him, how close he did not know until he dropped completely exhausted over the line as his ankles were grabbed.

Don Rutherford's shot at goal failed but what had looked like a certain Scottish victory had been turned into a 3–3 draw and Hancock had written himself into the record books as the scorer of a try from ninety-five yards out, the longest run-in of any scored in International rugby.

Andy Hancock played for Northampton and was a planner for Staffordshire County Council, and although his memorable try and that of Obolensky were radically different there was one respect in which the two men were similar. Hancock played in England's next International, bringing his total of appearances to three, but he was never picked again. Obolensky had achieved only four caps, so that the fame of these two England players rests not on a body of work for the national side but in each case on a never again repeated flash of brilliance.

Chapter 20

Twickenham's Round-the-Year Workers

Pending a move to new offices to be built in the East Car Park, the main offices of the Secretary of the Rugby Football Union, Air Commodore R. H. G. Weighill, and his staff of twenty-nine are under the West Stand just along the way from the committee rooms.

Bob Weighill's beautifully panelled mini-office has the plum corner site, with a view from one window of the main entrance gates and the other looking out over the West Concourse to the car park. He is the sixth paid secretary.

In 1904, after half a dozen honorary secretaries had held the post since the founding of the Rugby Union in 1871, it was realised that the job was too demanding for part-time work and Percy Coles, an Eastbourne solicitor and Sussex cricketer, became rugby's first 'professional'. At the old offices of the RFU at 35 Surrey Street, off the Strand, he had as staff a grand total of one clerk and after a mere three years packed it in to go fruit-farming in British Columbia.

A really great character, C. J. B. Marriott, formerly a school master, took over in 1907. O. L. Owen, in his history of the Rugby Union, wrote: 'One should not forget one most important, if for a while severely limited, piece of accommodation, the new Secretary's office at the southern end of the West Stand. Out of this exploded from time to time that remarkable personality, C. J. B. Marriott. Only those who realised what a warm heart beat inside the still husky frame of this irascible old Blue and former England forward ventured to accost him while in the pursuit of his duties. It required a brave man to beard him in his den.'

Marriott it was who saw through the construction and successful opening of Twickenham and he stayed on to complete seventeen years in office, retiring in that peak year for English rugby – 1924, with England grand-slam Champions for the second year running. Although then sixty-three the bowler-hatted, walrus-moustached Marriott did

C. J. B. Marriott, dynamic Secretary of the Rugby Union 1907–24, with Fred Stokes, first ever captain of England in 1871 (right).

not withdraw to his manorial estate of Fleed Hall in Sussex. He commuted regularly to the City, where he embarked on a fresh career in finance.

His successor, Engineer Commander Sydney F. Coopper RN, was the spectacular England wing who, at the turn of the century, captivated his home crowds by solving the problem of being confronted with a defender on his way to the goal line by jumping over him. Coopper

The RFU's longest serving Secretary (1924–47), Engineer Commander Sydney F. Coopper RN, was not above doing a bit of crowd packing on International days.

has been dubbed 'the father of modern Twickenham', since it was during his twenty-three years in office, up to 1947, that the additions and improvements were made which gave the ground the look it has today.

F. D. (Doug) Prentice, who took over from Coopper, was equally well known on the rugby field but not necessarily for England, for whom he gained only three caps in 1928. He captained the Lions on their 1930 tour of Australia and New Zealand, proving himself a great off-the-field diplomat when the outspoken manager, Major James Baxter, was at loggerheads with the New Zealand authorities over the conduct of the game in the then Dominion.

In 1962 Doug Prentice became ill – his duties were taken over by D. H. Harrison and Assistant Secretary Alfred Wright, who joined the staff in 1920 and is now archivist to the Rugby Union. He has made a start in assembling a rugby library and what is hoped will eventually be a museum. This is something in which the RFU lags sadly behind the MCC, with its fascinating museum behind the pavilion at Lord's. At the moment the RFU library consists merely of two rooms at 180 Whitton Road, where Wright is busily engaged in cataloguing thousands of old and modern rugby programmes and handbooks, leaflets, maps, photographs and books. The museum as yet is merely a pipe dream but eventually, it is hoped, historic jerseys and caps, footballs, trophies and other *memorabilia* will all be brought together in a building which could be put up somewhere on the Twickenham property and which would make a wonderful gift to the RFU from a well-to-do supporter!

In 1963 the new Secretary was R. E. Prescott, England front-row forward of the 1930s and son of the twenty-third President of the RFU. He was himself in line to be elected President, which would have been the first example of father and son holding the office, but instead he 'turned pro', as he put it, and took on the appointment of Secretary.

Bob Weighill took over in 1973. He was born in 1920 and went to the same school as Harold Wilson – Wirral Grammar School. He left school at sixteen to enter the Cheshire County Constabulary but his career in the police was ended by the war. In 1941 he joined the RAF with Fighter Command and remained in the service right through to his taking over the secretaryship at Twickenham. He was awarded the DFC in 1944. He commanded various operational units at home and abroad and his final post was Commandant, Royal Air Force, Halton. He was appointed ADC to the Queen in 1968.

Weighill fits in with what is now the tradition that the Secretary should be a former England player. He gained four caps as a forward in 1947 and 1948, the last, against France in Paris, as captain. Starting with his school team, it has invariably been as captain that he has turned out for a wide variety of sides, a reflection of his numerous different postings with the RAF. He has played for Birkenhead Park, Waterloo, Harlequins and Leicester and is among the select who have worn the Barbarians' jersey. He was captain of the RAF from 1945 to 1952, of Combined Services, Cheshire and Notts, Lincs and Derby. He was an England selector 1959–64.

He is a very experienced administrator and unflappable, which is an essential for this job which is now vastly more complex than in the old Surrey Street days. He has to keep a watchful eye on everything from schools rugby to Internationals and tours; the care and maintenance of Twickenham ('Are the new aluminium benches being installed in the enclosures just right for their function?'); RFU committee meetings, sub-committees, the International Board; royal and other VIP visits to headquarters; tickets and finances. Through it all Bob Weighill is found to be courteous and understanding, with a nice dry sense of humour which is helpful when confronted with the niggling little problems that constantly crop up. For instance you have all the seating arrangements finalised for the formal dinner of welcome

Air Commodore Bob Weighill (centre), present Secretary, with Don Rutherford (left) one of the two Assistant Secretaries, and John Burgess, appointed England coach in 1974.

for the Tongan tourists when at the last minute you are told that Miss Tonga would feel hurt if she were not there. *And* her chaperone. (They made it.)

One might have thought that when summer comes Air Commodore Weighill and his staff could indulge in pleasant off-season relaxation. That is not the case at all. No sooner has the rugby season finished than the auditors move in for a six-week visit. All the paper work has to be done for the Annual General Meeting in July. New editions of RFU publications for the following season have to be prepared and got off to press. The thousands of ticket-application forms have to be sent out, and innumerable other chores have to be done. It can truthfully be said that Weighill, his two Assistant Secretaries – Colonel T. D. Morgan, formerly of the Marines, on the administrative side, and Don Rutherford on the technical – and the rest at the Twickenham offices are as busy in the summer as they are in the winter.

Even the ground itself and the car parks are not deserted in summer. Twickenham plays host to such things as the Police Gala Day and school sports. When the circus comes to town the big top goes up in the North Car Park. And the Jehovah Witnesses for many years now have held their annual rally there. Apparently one thing that appeals to those good people in the choice of Twickenham for their get-together and the dunking of adherents in a big water tank set up in front of the West Stand, is that Twickenham, with its 186, has more toilets than any other sports ground in Britain.

Besides the paid staff at Twickenham there is another important group of workers.

Under the centre of the South Terrace there is a private restaurant and if you reach the ground well before the start of a match and happen to look in at one of the windows you will see more than a hundred men sitting down to lunch. The tables are neatly laid, with red checked tablecloths. There is a bar in one corner. Waitresses serve the customers from the printed menus of the best meal to be had at Twickenham. On the menu there is no mention of any charge. It is in fact free, because the people obviously enjoying it are the stewards, who will shortly be going on duty all around the stands at Twickenham.

There are 190 of them for an International, 130 at the Varsity Match, taking tickets and seeing that you get to your seat safely, standing at the entrances to the committee rooms, the Internationals' Bar, the dressing-rooms, the press box and other key points where they welcome those entitled to be in there and are politely dissuasive to those who are not.

Jehovah's Witnesses pack the stands for their annual get-together – one of the few summer events at Twickenham.

Their work is voluntary, which is the reason for the generously served lunch. The complimentary ticket they receive for each match looks different from those bought by the general public. Perforated down the middle and labelled on one side LUNCH and on the other TEA, it is torn in half and surrendered per meal. Besides being unpaid, they get no expenses whatsoever, despite the fact that some of them come from as far afield as Exeter, Gloucester and Cheshire. Even their own tie, a monogram of the initials of Rugby Union Steward on a green background, which they wear with pride, they have to buy themselves.

Yet when you talk to these men, who are in the charge of the chief steward Lieut-Col. J. B. Williams, and ask how long they have been doing it, it is not out of the ordinary to receive an answer like 'I started in 1938'. And such is their dedication, so much a reflection of the amateur spirit of rugby, that if you had thoughts of applying for the job of steward at Twickenham you can forget it. It is not done by application. You have to be nominated by a steward of long standing and then, if the nomination is accepted, you go on to a four-year waiting list!

In addition to the stewards there are 40 'ground keepers' dotted around Twickenham during a big match to look after ground control. The system, which started with the Barbarians' match against New Zealand in November 1974, was worked out with appropriate military efficiency by Assistant Secretary Colonel Morgan. The ground is divided into sections, each batch of stewards having a group commander with a walkie-talkie with which he can keep in constant touch with Colonel Morgan, master-minding the whole operation from a 'boat' high up between the Upper and Lower West Stand. Beside him sits a police officer who similarly keeps in touch with policemen on duty inside and outside the ground. Between them they watch out for every sort of eventuality such as spectators trying to invade the field, any disturbance that might crop up, or a casualty who may need attention from the ambulancemen. Twickenham is the only rugby ground to have instituted this smooth-working system of crowd control.

Chapter 21

The Demo Season

Undoubtedly the most unusual season at Twickenham, one productive of extraordinary scenes, was that of the tour of the 1969–70 Springboks.

In view of the fanatical anti-apartheid feelings in various quarters, there was agitation that the tour be called off, but the British rugby authorities adhered to the view that politics should not be mixed with sport. They refused to bow to the agitators, who would have regarded it as a fine show of power if they had been able to dictate to the Rugby Football Union and the other Home Unions. To the admiration of the rugby public, those in charge of the tour expressed their determination to carry it through, no matter what efforts the hotheads might make to disrupt it.

From the moment their plane arrived at Heathrow the Springboks were kicked at, spat upon and reviled. Demonstrators lay down on the street outside their hotel to try to prevent their team coach from moving off, and pestered them wherever they went in London. A couple of days before their first match, against Oxford University, they mysteriously moved out of the city, but not to Oxford or anywhere near there. The fixture, as far as Oxford as a venue was concerned, had been cancelled since it had not been felt possible adequately to safeguard Iffley Road from demonstrations. Would the match in fact ever be held and if so where?

I happened to be with them at their hide-out in the Dormy Hotel in Ferndale, on the outskirts of Bournemouth, because I was writing a book on the tour, and as we whiled away the time there, with uniformed police and dog-handlers outside the hotel and plainclothesmen mingling with the guests inside, nobody except the team management and top Rugby Union officials knew precisely what was being planned. Not until eleven o'clock on the night before the scheduled fixture was it announced that the game was on – at Twickenham.

Right after breakfast the convoy started off on the 100-mile trip to London, the team coach in front, a police car next with its long radio aerial swaying back and forth, and bringing up the rear the press coach, in which some English was to be heard every now and then intermingled with the Afrikaans.

Just near Camberley we left the main road and drove into a secluded spot in the woods. There were three reasons for the halt. The players went off for little solo walks among the trees. Hampers were brought forth from the boot of the team coach and a superb picnic lunch provided by the hotel was enjoyed. And then there was the little ceremony of the handing over of police responsibility for the team by the Hampshire and Dorset detectives to the Surrey constabulary.

Now that we were nearing Twickenham, on which the demonstrators were naturally going to converge, police protection was intensified. We took the road again with not just one squad car but three – one in front, one between the two coaches and one at the back, supported by motor-cycle outriders. One could not help but feel that this was the strangest manner in which a touring team had ever set off for its opening match.

Stranger still was the scene at the ground when the convoy made its way slowly through the hordes of demonstrators outside waving their banners and their fists at the Springboks, to the West Car Park, where there was such an assemblance of mounted police that somebody remarked: 'Ye gods, Balaclava!' The West Concourse, where friends normally congregate for a chat before the match, now looked like a police parade ground. No spectators had yet been allowed inside. Only police, 540 of them to be precise, lined up receiving their instructions as to how they would be deployed.

When the spectators were allowed in – by invitation or at 5s a head at the turnstiles – they were restricted to the West Stand and the standing enclosures in front of it. The remainder of the ground was sealed off with stout wire-netting, patrolled by police. The stands and terraces on the north, east and south looked depressingly empty, the only sign of life being the little oasis of the press box in the centre of the East Stand, which the correspondents had been allowed to use because of the telephone and other facilities there. To get to it one had to be vetted by the batches of police who had now taken their places in cordons around each entrance to the empty terraces. Just before reaching the door leading up to the press box was a high wire-netting barricade which looked impassable. I bumped into a correspondent coming away to go and have a look at the situation outside the ground and he told me: 'You can get in easily enough. There's a steward on duty there. The password's "Mind your nut".' I did not quite know what he meant until I reached the wire-netting and the steward, bending down to pull up a gap in it for me, said, 'Mind your nut!'

The concentration camp atmosphere of wire-netting and police prompted the *Morning Star* to comment afterwards: 'It was proved that it is possible for white-to-white rugby contact to be maintained if the stadium is turned into a Police state.'

The crowd, which totalled 10,000 by the kick-off, were herded into the West Stand and enclosure with a steel mesh barricade between them and the field, and along the entire length of the touchline was a phalanx of shoulder-to-shoulder policemen – facing the crowd in American style, which is not normally the British way. A Rugby Union official, mindful of the fact that more than a few robust rugby types in the crowd would have liked to have got at the demonstrators, announced over the public address system: 'The pitch is out of bounds and will you please leave any control to our friends the police.'

The Springboks advent on the field was greeted by a barrage of 'Sieg Heil!', 'Fascist pigs!' and 'Go home, Springboks, go home', sung to the tune of 'We're Here Because We're Here'. The demonstrators, clearly with thoughts of invading the pitch, had concentrated themselves at the front of the enclosure, where they joined in slow handclaps and the blowing of many referees' whistles which was to confuse those there to watch rugby but oddly enough not the players. So efficient was the police cordon that only two demonstrators managed to get on to the field. One youth made for the goal posts at one end and tried to climb them but he was soon escorted off. At half-time a middle-aged man clad like a rugby coach seemed to appear from nowhere and went unnoticed on the field until the referee was about to start the second half and he was seen to be standing beside him. Police came on to lead him quietly away.

They dealt more sternly with demonstrators when trouble broke out among the spectators packing the enclosure. The police hauled them over the barricade and frog-marched them off through the players' tunnel. One put up such a fight that it required four policemen holding, one at each leg and the other two holding his arms, before he could be removed. The rugby fans recognised him as Peter Hain and loudly applauded his exit.

Strangely enough the incessant anti-Springbok chanting of the agitators subsided as the match was reaching its late stages and there seemed to be only one explanation for this. Oxford were in the lead and were playing so well that it looked as though they were going to record a sensational upset by beating the tourists in their very first match. It appeared that the demonstrators realised that they had failed in their aim of sabotaging the match or even disrupting what was happening on the field and had settled for the pleasure of seeing the, to them, hated South Africans beaten.

The master-mind of what was to turn out to be a historic 6–3 victory

Removing non-players from the field so that the match between the Springboks and London Counties can get under way during the South Africans' 'demo tour' of 1969–70.

for Oxford was their captain, Chris Laidlaw, who completely outshone his illustrious rival Dawie de Villiers and inspired his team mates to carry out with expertise all the All Black techniques of rucking and the like in which he had coached them. With such verve and application did the Oxford pack of unknowns rise to the occasion against experienced campaigners like Du Preez, Greyling and Myburgh that at the final whistle they were so spent that at least one of them – Peter Dixon, who was to get an England cap mainly through his performance in this match – had no strength left to leap in the air and merely rolled around on the ground with joy.

Not to detract from a famous victory, it should be said in fairness to the tourists that it is not the best of mental preparation for a match to arrive at the ground two hours before kick-off and have to hang around for that time when an hour is regarded by players as just the right amount of time to get ready and in the mood. And it did not help them at all to be told just before they ran out on to the field: 'Make sure you have your overcoats handy, to cover up your Springbok gear if things get out of hand and you have to make a quick getaway.'

From the experience of this, their first attempt to stage a match in the face of demonstrators' announced intention to wreck it, the Rugby Union was able to have Twickenham looking less like a prisoner-of-war camp for their next match of the 'demo season'. The 30,000 spectators for London Counties' game against the tourists were allowed to take their places in most of the normal seating and although there were hold-ups from time to time through invasions of the pitch, the match was completed as scheduled. The star-studded London side was fully expected to repeat successes of their forerunners against the Springboks. And why not, with seven Internationals on board, including J. P. R. Williams at full-back, centres John Dawes and Bob Lloyd, and on one wing Bob Hiller, selected in that odd position for him because of his place-kicking. In the event, however, they appeared badly coached and were easily overrun by the Springboks 22–6.

London Counties were in fact something of a rabble and the unfortunate picture they presented was added to by a foolish idea on somebody's part that Hiller could not be expected to shine as a running wing, so he was given the throw-ins to do for all London line-outs no matter on which side of the field they were. Seldom have such farcical goings-on been seen at Twickenham as Hiller, over on the right wing, forgot he was supposed to switch for throw-ins with left wing Bulpitt when it was London's ball on the other side of the field, and captain John Dawes had to give him the hurry-up sign to run across and get on with the job.

The police contingent having been increased to 800 for the London match, a further 50 were recruited when a normal-looking crowd was on hand for the England match. England, captained by Bob Hiller, happily returned to his full-back role, were playing their first match under the newly introduced squad system with a coach, Don White, and when South Africa took an early 8-point lead through a penalty by Visagie and his conversion of a Greyling try, the diehards who had been against such 'professional' preparation were heard to be crowing: 'See – going against the true spirit of the game doesn't work.'

However, just on half-time a brilliant sequence of inter-passing by England started by scrum-half Starmer-Smith to his partner Shackleton saw the ball going in rapid succession to forwards Bucknall, Larter and Fairbrother and then back to Larter for an exciting try.

In the second half Hiller kicked a penalty and then when there was a scramble on the South African line Pullin touched down after Dawie de Villiers seemed convinced he had already made the ball dead. Hiller converted to make it an 11–8 lead for England, which they held on to until the bitter end while the crowd, wild with excitement, saw them survive no fewer than four let-offs – an easy penalty which the referee reversed when a Springbok forward addressed a comment to him, a missed Visagie drop from in front of the posts, a kick over the England line which Lawless could not beat to the dead-ball line and a disallowed try by Tony Roux.

It was a justly earned first-ever victory by England over South Africa, for by that stage of their tour the Springboks had become hardened to demonstrations and nothing happened anyway during this match which could have been said to have detracted from their concentration.

For Twickenham's final match of the demo season of 1969–70, the Barbarians versus the tourists, the police attendance was stepped up to 1,500. Although it might seem to be, this was not a record, since there had been no fewer than 2,300 policemen on hand for South Africa's match against Ireland, Irish troubles having been an extra consideration. The reason for the increase in security forces at Twickenham was that the demonstrators had quite failed to prevent any of the twenty-three matches so far from being completed. (The cancellation of the Belfast fixture against Ulster, rearranged as a match against New Brighton and North of Ireland at Leasowe, Cheshire, was because of domestic difficulties.) So the demonstrators had announced an all-out effort to wreck the last match of the tour against the Baa-baas.

The throwing of tacks and drawing-pins on to the pitch had become a new technique developed by the anti-apartheid hotheads and this was offset at Twickenham by sweeping the turf with magnets. Smoke bombs were thrown during the course of the match but the volume of smoke they produced was sparse, they were easily stamped out and were of little effect in preventing the 25,000 crowd from watching what was an easy 21–12 win for the Springboks.

Chapter 22

Life in the Press Box

It is a tradition of the press box that no emotion is shown in regard to what is happening on the field. A sensational 75-yard try, a gigantic 60-yard penalty, a match-winning drop-kick in the dying seconds, all these must be viewed but not applauded or cheered. This deadpan reaction to events no doubt stemmed originally from a desire on the part of the gentlemen of the press to let those in a position to observe them at work see that their attitude was impartial, unbiased and in all ways fair.

It is amusing to see a new boy in the press box indicate to all around that he is a fledgling by jumping up and clapping when the first exciting thing happens, suddenly to realise that none of the other writers are doing it and shamefacedly sit down again. But newcomers should not be too worried about such gaffes. On more occasions than one the oldtimers in the Twickenham press box have been seen to be quite incapable of restraining the natural urge to join the paying spectators around them in unfettered applause. I remember the excited cheering and pounding of their desks at the sheer brilliance of the action in the Barbarians match with the All Blacks in 1967, and when Mervyn Davies scored the try which brought the scores level in the same fixture in 1974, above the roar of the crowd could be heard an almighty crack as half the perspex rain guard in the front row came adrift from its moorings, which could hardly have been done by a sudden gust of wind.

There are 107 seats in the press box at Twickenham, which seems a goodly amount of accommodation. But when it is the England–Wales match, the biggest drawcard of the home Internationals, or another showpiece such as the fixture against a topnotch touring side, it is a taxing time for Terry Cooper, of the Press Association, whose job it is, with the authority of the RFU, to allocate those 107 places. He is inundated with all sorts of applications from fringe types such as the chief rugby correspondent of *Old Moore's Almanack*. Many are disappointed as the space is restricted to regular journalists.

The take-off for the devastating Duckham side-step with which Roland Bertranne was clearly not going to be able to cope in the England–France charity match in 1974.

Everybody who has been to Twickenham knows what the press box, in the centre of the lower East Stand, looks like from outside – the rows of orange-coloured wooden desks, with perspex shields in front to stop the rain which tends to drift in there from setting ball-point notes awash. But few know of the rugby writers' own little world down the little flight of steps to the innards of the stand. It is a very agreeable set-up, the like of which is not to be found at the other Home Union venues. (Murrayfield does have something of the same, but lacking in one very important ingredient.) There are two rooms with spacious tables for writing. There are twelve telephone booths, with five other phones dotted around. There is a well-appointed washroom, a buffet and bar (this last being what the Scots lack).

Life in the Press Box

When the final whistle goes the place immediately becomes jam-packed. The correspondents of the Sunday papers, the news agencies and the overseas press go into feverish action at the writing tables and it would be a brave man who would dare to engage any of them in conversation. The daily paper men, whose stories do not appear until the Monday, and others without pressing deadlines head straight for the bar, to be armed with a drink while they circulate in the lobby or cluster up over a post mortem of the game, all the time mentally writing their stories and making adjustments to their assessment of the match if somebody comes up with an acute observation. For certain uncrowded matches a notice is put on the wall to the effect that wives and offspring, girl friends and chums may be admitted to the inner sanctum after the game. Family company always adds a certain *je ne sais quoi* to a predominantly male scene, and the young sons, munching their pork pies and sausage rolls while waiting for Dad to finish his story or his drinking, are always obviously tickled pink by the fact that when they return to school not only will they be able to say that they saw the big match but that afterwards they rubbed shoulders with such luminaries of the rugby writing world as Vivian Jenkins, John Reason, David Frost, Barry John and the Thomases, Clem and J.B.G.

There is a camaraderie in the press box which ensures that an old pals' act operates when something happens on the field that nobody can quite follow. Who was the scorer after that scramble on the line? What was the exact sequence of that slick inter-passing which led to a try? What was the offence the referee whistled up to give England this vital penalty shot? Comments are exchanged and the facts established, on the basis that you do not mind in the least if your opposition gets it wrong, but you have a nagging thought in the back of your mind that you might get it wrong yourself. However, in recent years, another aid to accuracy has been a portable television set in the front row of the press box, next to John Reason.

In the past the press box at Twickenham has had its doyens such as O. L. Owen of *The Times*, 'Dai' Gent of *The Sunday Times* and H. B. Toft of *The Observer*. In the 1970s among the established regulars is the former Oxford, Wales and Lions full-back Vivian Jenkins, of *The Sunday Times*: a big man in all respects, as anyone who has sat beside him in the box can confirm, he could be regarded as the dean of the rugby writers, like Jim Swanton at Lord's. Also, formerly of Wales and the Lions but as a forward, there is Clem Thomas of *The Observer* and the meat business in Swansea, whose wit and neat turn of phrase in his reports is very much in evidence, too, in the press box. John Reason is *The Daily Telegraph* man, an assiduous student of the game,

Arguably the world's greatest wing in the 1970s, Gerald Davies, shadowed by Jeremy Janion, in the England–Wales clash of 1972.

who knows more about and writes more about what happens in the front row than any of them. The quiet-spoken David Frost, of the *Guardian*, is there, with his sound judgements and incisive comment placing him among the best of the correspondents. He always looks back with amusement to when, already firmly established as a rugby writer, he received a communication from a young man named David Frost, just down from Cambridge and seeking fame in the world of television, suggesting that to avoid confusion he (the rugby Frost) should change his by-line. The popular J. B. G. (Bryn) Thomas, chief

A great day for the Irish: Kevin Flynn streaks over for Ireland's winning try in the last minute of their 1972 International at Twickenham. Mike Gibson is happily in support, Alan Old not so happy.

rugby writer for the *Western Mail* and the author of numerous rugby books, is at every match wearing the distinctive check cap which places no obscurity upon his whereabouts – very knowledgeable about the game, especially Welsh rugby, and if you know about Welsh rugby, what else do you need to know? Affable, anecdotal Pat Marshall, of the *Daily Express*, was another of the regulars who always seemed to be happy at his work. Terry O'Connor, of the *Daily Mail*, is another, and probably the best of them all at getting material over and above what happens on the field. When he sniffs a good story of that type

Newly capped (in 1974) Terry Cobner shows the aggressive type of loose forward play which made him a valuable regular for Wales. In this England match he has eluded Ripley and does not seem to need colleagues Llewellyn, Mervyn Davies and Delme Thomas.

he goes at it with the true instinct of a newshound. Terry McLean, of the *New Zealand Herald* and author of good rugby books, is seen only when the All Blacks are here but is highly respected as one of the world's top rugby correspondents. A self-confessed 'cantankerous cuss', one always feels that there is a nice chap inside trying to get out. And of course the rugby writers always like to see Peter West come dancing into the press box to do his report for *The Times*.

Chapter 23

The Baa-baas Come to Twickenham

The now traditional final match of major touring teams against the Barbarians started in 1948, when it was arranged as an extra fixture at Cardiff Arms Park for the Australians, who had come to the end of their tour a bit short financially. That opportunity for British rugby fans to see something resembling a Lions side in action at home was such a success that it became a regular Cardiff attraction, always hugely and enthusiastically attended. But three times now, for special reasons, the venue has been switched to Twickenham – for the 1967 All Blacks, the 1969–70 Springboks and the 1974 All Blacks.

BARBARIANS *v.* ALL BLACKS
16 December 1967

It was foot-and-mouth disease, of all things, which brought the black-and-white striped Barbarians, founded in 1890 to play merely against leading clubs, on their first major visit to Twickenham. The 1967 All Blacks' fixture list of eighteen matches in Canada, the British Isles and France had been cut by the two Irish matches because of an outbreak of the disease on that island. I remember Colin Meads telling me that so worried were they in New Zealand about the possibility of its being brought back by the team on their return that all their playing equipment – jerseys, shorts, boots, footballs, everything – were to be burnt before they boarded their homeward plane. I kicked myself afterwards for not asking him to hold back his gear and a couple of footballs from the holocaust and give them to me; what a wonderful conversation piece they would have made among my rugby souvenirs.

To compensate for the loss of two fixtures with this great All Black team of whom everybody wanted to see more, it was hurriedly decided to add another game at the end of their tour, against the Baa-baas, a fixture not originally scheduled since this was not regarded as a 'major' tour. The Cardiff Arms Park fans, having already had the pleasure of their company for two matches, as against Twickenham's mere one, it was decided to break with tradition and stage the match at England's HQ.

When I settled my wife and young son in the North Stand before going around to the press box I figured that they were going to be a bit lonely, for there were only about half a dozen other people with them in the tiers of empty seats. The final crowd amounted to 40,000; more than 30,000 short of capacity at Twickenham, this was not quite in keeping with the way they flock to this fixture in Cardiff. The attendance was disappointing but those who had not come to swell it to capacity were disappointed, because they missed what turned out to be one of the most exciting matches ever seen at Twickenham.

The teams were:

Barbarians: S. Wilson (Scotland, capt.); R. E. Webb (England), T. G. R. Davies (Wales), R. H. Lloyd (England), W. K. Jones (Wales); B. John (Wales), G. Edwards (Wales); G. A. Sherriff (England), J. P. Fisher (Scotland), M. Wiltshire (Wales), P. J. Larter (England), R. B. Taylor (England), C. H. Norris (Wales), F. A. L. Laidlaw (Scotland), A. L. Horton (England).

All Blacks: W. F. McCormick; M. J. Dick, W. L. Davis, A. G. Steel; I. R. MacRae, E. W. Kirton; C. R. Laidlaw; B. J. Lochore (capt.), K. R. Tremain, C. E. Meads, S. C. Strahan, W. J. Nathan, B. L. Muller, B. E. McLeod, K. F. Gray.

Referee: M. Joseph (Wales).

When the All Blacks took the field there was a standing ovation for this team schooled by Fred Allen, a coach of the same stature as Carwyn James. It was an acknowledgement by the crowd of the All Blacks having brought New Zealand rugby to one of its highest peaks, before the sad decline into which it slipped on their next visit to Britain.

From the start both teams gave every indication that the match was going to be played in the true tradition of open Baa-baa rugby. The touchline was treated as though there lurked the dread foot-and-mouth. The ball was thrown about with abandon and any kicks were upfield rather than to touch. Stewart Wilson fielded one of them just inside the All Blacks' half and opened the scoring with a superb 45-yard drop. Barbarians 3, All Blacks 0.

The All Black slickness developed on tour ('Spin it! Spin it!' Fred Allen used to scream at them in training) was now very much in evidence but oddly lacking in finish by inexcusable dropping of final passes on a dry summer-like day. Kirton seemed to despair of sending it out only for it eventually to be mishandled, and he grabbed points where he could by dropping a goal from thirty yards out. Barbarians 3, All Blacks 3.

Cardiff's midfield trio of that time – Gareth Edwards, Barry John and Gerald Davies – had given the All Blacks a lot of trouble on the previous Wednesday, when they had been the root cause of the tourists being held to a draw by East Wales, the only smudge on their unbeaten record. Now they were at it again, ably assisted by Bob Lloyd, the Harlequins centre, who had also proved himself a thorn in the All Blacks' side with three tries against them, one for the Midlands and two for England.

But although these penetrating Barbarian backs were not suffering from their opponents' temporary lapse into mishandling, they lacked support when they made their breaks. The Baa-baas' loose forwards, in their following up, just did not have the dazzling mobility of such as Waka Nathan and Kel Tremain.

So, despite the excitement of back and forth play up and down the field, neither side was able to augment its score by the time the interval came.

Half-time: Barbarians 3, All Blacks 3.

Before what can only be called the big finish there were three magnificent runs, first by the Baa-baa right wing Keri Jones, then by Gerald Davies and the third by Waka Nathan, which had the crowd yelling their enthusiasm and, very unusually, the writers in the press box jumping to their feet and cheering and pounding the desks with their fists to swell the applause.

The Keri Jones break took him from half way deep into the All Blacks' 25 with Davies inside him and only Fergie McCormick to beat. But the wily New Zealand full-back forced him to hesitate and delay too long a pass to Davies, and instead he kicked ahead, alas too far, over the deadball line.

The runaway by Gerald Davies was along practically the same route and again with a man beside him when McCormick loomed up in front. It was a tribute to the tough little All Black full-back that again he was able to block a 'certain' try, crowding Davies and his colleague so that Davies could not get an effective pass to him.

It was almost immediately afterwards that Waka Nathan got possession near the All Blacks' line and set off on a devastating run along the other side of the field which took him into the Barbarians' 25 before Wilson managed to nail him.

Things were happening so fast that in the press box a correspondent whose report would not appear until the Monday was heard to say: 'I can't get it all down. I'll have to read about it tomorrow.'

Wedged in between the runs by Jones and Davies was the move that brought the most thunderous applause of all. Barry John weaved his way through a cluster of defenders in midfield and then put in a well-directed kick towards the left corner flag. It was covered by the New Zealanders moving back but, whether a stroke of genius by John or just fortuitously, the ball abruptly stopped dead – and the cover defence kept going on the route it should rightfully have taken. Bob Lloyd, following up, had nothing to do but pick it up and dot it over the line for a total of four personal tries scored against the tourists. Barbarians 6, All Blacks 3.

Despite all the crowd-thrilling activity that followed, that was the way the score stayed, the Baa-baas hanging on resolutely to their lead, as the clock showed that full time had been reached and the Twickhamists keyed up for the ovation they would give the home team when the final whistle went and the unbeaten record of the 1967 All Blacks had been broken at last.

But the All Blacks' left wing, Tony Steel, who was New Zealand 100- and 220-yard sprint champion, set out to prove that he had determination as well as speed. From a scrum on his side of the field he came into the line between half-back and first five-eighth and proceeded to barge his way through the defence in a diagonal run which took him to within a matter of yards from the Baa-baas' line. There someone managed to grab his jersey and as he swivelled around, brought to earth, he tossed the ball up to MacRae, whom nobody could stop from getting over.

Would McCormick's shot at goal convert it from a 6–6 draw to a victory for the All Blacks? He missed and everybody said, 'Oh well, a draw is a fair result', which nobody ever means sincerely, especially in this case, with the Baa-baas having the game in the bag at full time and then having to settle for a draw in extra time.

But while the crowd were doing this musing the game was on again. It was now four minutes into injury time when Wilson fielded the ball on his 25 in front of the posts. There was no one near him with whom he could mount an attack so he had no choice but to kick to touch, after which the final whistle would surely go.

He started left and then changed his mind, to kick to the right-hand touchline. He was probably off balance when he kicked, for he miscued – right into the arms of Brian Lochore, with Kirton and Steel outside him and only Keri Jones between them and the goal line.

The onlookers could only pray that the All Blacks' dropped passes of earlier in the game would be repeated but the prayers were un-

Climax to one of the great Barbarians matches at Twickenham: Tony Steel outdistances Gerald Davies and Keri Jones to score the winning try in injury time, to the glee of Meads, Waka Nathan and Kirton.

availing and Steel sailed across. McCormick converted. The whistle went.

Final score: Barbarians 6, All Blacks 11.

It was bitterly disappointing to have come so close but the crowd stayed to cheer what had been one of the great matches of Twickenham, as Lochore was traditionally shouldered off the field as captain at the end of his team's tour. The match ended with the other tradition established in Cardiff for this fixture: they sang *Auld Lang Syne* and *Now Is the Hour*, although it was not done, one must confess, with the same sort of fervour and volume encountered at the Arms Park, but this was the first time the Twickenham fans had been called upon to do it and, after all, the English do not have the same admirable lack of self-consciousness as the Welsh in such matters.

BARBARIANS v. SPRINGBOKS
31 January 1970

In 1970 at Cardiff Arms Park they were busy building that magnificent half of a National Stadium so it was thought best to switch the Barbarians v. Springboks match of that year to Twickenham. Present were 25,000 and 1,500 policemen, since it was that notorious demo tour. The match was won comfortably by the Springboks, 21–12, and was memorable for a superb 60-yard try by David Duckham which was later used in the regular opening scenes for the BBC's 'Rugby Special' programme, and another solo effort equally as good by Jan Ellis, which was not.

BARBARIANS v. ALL BLACKS
30 November 1974

This was undoubtedly the most excitedly awaited match at Twickenham for many a year. When the 1967 All Blacks had met the Barbarians at Twickenham the injury-time 11–6 win by the New Zealanders had provided one of the most exciting games ever seen at the ground. It was topped by their 1973 fixture at Cardiff, described not without justification as 'the greatest rugby match ever played'. Could they do it again?

For months before the match at pubs and at rugby clubs and anywhere else where rugbymen got together the all-important date of 30 November would crop up: 'It might turn out to be an awful flop'; 'It all depends, what the Baa-baa selectors should do is pick the Lions Test side'; 'They can't, because there's the tradition that there must be one uncapped player'; so the conversation ran. Then when the Barbarian team was announced, with its compromise of the entire Lions Test pack, there was a further upsurge of interest. Then came the All Blacks' unbeaten short tour of Ireland and their match against Wales masquerading as a Welsh XV. Then the news that the match was a sell-out. Such a state of anticipation was reached that perhaps it was inaccurate to say that it was the most excitedly awaited match at Twickenham for many a year; it was, rather, the most excitedly awaited match there ever.

The teams:

Barbarians: A. R. Irvine (Heriot's FP and Scotland); T. G. R. Davies (Cardiff and Wales), P. J. Warfield (Cambridge and England), P. S. Preece (Coventry and England), D. J. Duckham (Coventry and England); J. D. Bevan (Aberavon), G. O. Edwards (Cardiff and Wales); J. McLaughlan (Jordanhill and Scotland), R. W. Windsor (Pontypool and

Wales), F. E. Cotton (Coventry and England), W. J. McBride (Ballymena and Ireland, capt.), G. L. Brown (West of Scotland and Scotland), R. M. Uttley (Gosforth and England), J. S. Slattery (Blackrock College and Ireland), T. M. Davies (Swansea and Wales).

All Blacks: J. F. Karam; B. G. Williams, B. J. Robertson, G. B. Batty; I. A. Hurst, D. J. Robertson; S. M. Going; K. K. Lambert, R. W. Norton, K. J. Tanner, P. J. Whiting, H. H. MacDonald, I. A. Kirkpatrick, K. W. Stewart, A. R. Leslie (capt.).

Referee: G. Domercq (France).

Did the match live up to this terrific advance publicity?

The 72,000 onlookers in sunny, ideal conditions saw a great game of rugby football of a quality far above the average International. But one could not escape a tinge of disappointment. It soon became evident that one team was playing traditional open Barbarian rugby – and it was not the Baa-baas. At one stage when Willie John McBride was injured and was receiving attention, a voice was heard: 'Take him off and let's get on with a real All Blacks–Baa-baas match!'

It seemed clear from the outset that McBride, with his Lions match-winning pack around him, wished to settle the whole matter up front. An indication of this was that the first scrum of the match – a clash of Titans – took an interminable time to get itself sufficiently organised for the ball to be put in. However, what was right for the Lions on tour in South Africa was wrong for Twickenham on this day. Willie John McBride, the greatest of the Lions captains, seemed to be playing Test rugby against a team willing and eager to fit in with the spirit of this famous fixture.

I could not help but be reminded of 1961 when the Barbarians had also departed from their avowed approach to the game, taking the field determined to 'do' the unbeaten Springboks in their last match, which they did, 6–0, through the stitching of the touchline by Richard Sharp and by other similar win-at-all-costs tactics. But then the situation had been altogether different. The surly South Africans had been unpopular and the British fans were right behind the Baa-baas in their intention to cut them down to size. On 30 November 1974, however, the All Blacks were not unpopular. In fact they had just won their way back into the hearts of the British as their favourite visitors by showing on their short tour of Ireland that they were all out to prove that their 1972–3 tour had been just a momentary fall from grace. Also, nobody could help but admire a team willing to take on the unprecedented task of playing what amounted to three Tests on a Saturday–Wednesday–Saturday basis – their Irish International, the Welsh XV match and now this game against the Barbarians.

Typical hoist by Sid Going, with captain Leslie and Kirkpatrick looking on approvingly in the All Blacks' keenly awaited 1974 match against the Baa-baas.

In such circumstances it cut right across the mood of the Twickenham crowd that McBride's intention appeared to be to play the ten-man game until the All Blacks had been subdued and then, but not until then, cut loose with true Baa-baa rugby.

In the event it did not work. The All Black forwards, with their own tradition of being great in the loose and at the ruck and now with newly developed expertise in the tight, were not to be subdued and it was only by what was regarded as the purest injustice that the Barbarians achieved the result they did.

From the kick-off we had the two indications of what was going to be the approach of the two sides: from the ensuing line-out New Zealand spun the ball right out along their back line; then at the first scrum the Barbarian/Lions pack fought and jostled so long for dominance that Going seemed to despair of ever being able to get the ball in.

The Baa-baas Come to Twickenham

There was no repetition of that sensational Baa-baa try in the opening stages of the 1973 match but five minutes into the game they did get points on the board. When Irvine kicked a high, true penalty from fifty yards the crowd reaction was quite loud by Twickenham standards – but it was nothing compared to the decibel count that greeted later events. Barbarians 3, All Blacks 0.

With the New Zealand backs running the ball at every opportunity they were unable to make that final breakthrough mainly because of the superb tackling and cover defence of centres Preece and Warfield, particularly the latter. He was of course in the team for that ability but as regards his other attribute – strong running – he was not to be seen throughout the match. It was not his fault. One is hard put to it to remember his ever receiving the ball from along the line at a set piece. Preece was also starved in this respect and the two very good breaks he did make were from a New Zealand handling error and an interception. The Barbarians were playing the Downing Street game – it must not go beyond No. 10.

Meanwhile the way the New Zealand backs were all tearing into it was indicated at one point when Grant Batty, the flying nugget, went so fast at Gerald Davies that when blocked he flew right over the wooden parapet into the crowd, a happening so rare at Twickenham that those who finished under him might well have been prompted to say, 'We're used to the ball landing on us, but this is ridiculous.'

After twenty-seven minutes Karam scored from an easy penalty when Irvine was caught in possession on his own 25 and there was an infringement in the ruck. Barbarians 3, All Blacks 3.

Then seven minutes later Gerald Davies, as if a little ashamed at being invited to Twickenham for a Baa-baas game and finding himself in a team under instructions to play Test rugby, decided to enter into the real spirit. The trouble was, though, that he did the right thing at the wrong time. In his own 25 near touch, with no support, he decided to run it – straight at a batch of unsmiling giants. From the moment the ruck formed a New Zealand try was on. They moved play up to the Baa-baas' line. From the new ruck there Going almost dived over and as a mêlée developed Leslie just bided his time until inevitably the ball came back for him to deposit it across the line. Barbarians 3, All Blacks 7.

Just before half-time the Baa-baas' fly-half, John Bevan, sliced through the New Zealand backs for an exciting run which took him from halfway to within yards of the line, only for his pass to be smothered by the defence. The only uncapped player on the field, this young man from Aberavon did not seem the least bit overawed by the company he was in and he could have been said to have been making

1. Merv (the Swerve) Davies scores his superb try for the Barbarians against the All Blacks in 1974. (1) With Gareth Edwards, Slattery and McBride in evidence behind him, he swerves outside Sid Going

3.

2.

and (2) inside Andy Leslie, taking a risk holding the ball in one hand but (3) keeping it away from Leslie's attempted smother tackle, to touch down (4) with Lamont a late-comer on the scene.

4.

an excellent debut had it been an International; the carefree Barbarian approach was not there.

Half-time: Barbarians 3, All Blacks 7.

The two teams had hardly settled into the second half before a New Zealand late tackle gave Irvine a 35-yard chance which he accepted gratefully (Barbarians 6, All Blacks 7) and then the tourists treated the crowd to some spectacular open play which they could not help but acclaim. One of the high spots was a run by Bryan Williams from deep inside his own half in which he seemed magically to dart right past tackler after tackler in midfield before eventually being brought down near the posts. The other was started by Batty fielding a high kick on his 25 and launching a sevens-type chuckabout among his colleagues before Going headed north and transferred to Kirkpatrick in the Baa-baas' half. A wonderful runner to watch, Kirkpatrick powered his way into the opposing 25 and, when inter-passing among the other forwards was in danger of breaking down, Peter Whiting raised himself to his full height and threw out a tremendous one-handed pass to Bryan Williams out on the right wing. The man with the tree-trunk thighs passed infield to Hurst when hemmed in by the corner flag. Hurst could not quite get there. From the ruck Going all but made it. He flicked to Leslie, who got over but did not quite touch down properly. The referee gave the down-spread arms sign that it was no score, despite a voice from the crowd: 'Oh, give it to them, it was so good!'

For their part, the Barbarians were not providing this sort of scintillating play. When the ball came deep into their territory they opted for the kick to touch, especially as executed by John Bevan. I found it ironic that Bevan, who was in the side because of the tradition that the Barbarians for this fixture always include an uncapped player, did not feel that he should also abide by the other Baa-baa tradition of 'the willingness to take risks', as Tony O'Reilly put it in his article in the match programme.

With fifteen minutes to go Andy Irvine dug his hole for a 55-yard penalty shot and when he goaled it, it struck me that I had never heard such an ovation at Twickenham. And so the Barbarians led the All Blacks 9–7, as much against the run of play as Joe Bugner outpointing Muhammad Ali.

Twelve, ten minutes to go and then . . .

The petulant Batty has made himself unpopular with British fans, but, to echo the feeling of many, you must hand it to him, he is good. There came a try now that was all his making. Going had kicked high ahead. Just as Irvine got under it, Batty was on top of him. From the ruck Going made a little break to another, at which Batty played scrum-half. When he got the ball, in a flash he directed a beautiful diagonal kick across the posts, far out to the Williams wing. It was so well placed behind Duckham that Williams had merely to breeze around him and collect, and after he had crossed the line all poor Duckham could do was grab his jersey to stop him rounding behind the posts. New Zealand oldtimers among the supporters over to watch the All Blacks' matches could not help but be reminded that once (and only once) New Zealand had had a truly great fly-half, Mark Nicholls by name, and this manoeuvre was pure Nicholls tactical genius displayed by a wing, of whom such things are not normally expected.

Karam, who uncharacteristically was to succeed with only one of four penalty attempts and then wave Leslie away when he offered him another, managed to convert the Williams try with an in-off from the left upright. Barbarians 9, All Blacks 13.

Justice had been done. But had it?

All of a sudden the Baa-baas started to throw the ball around, as if Willie John had said to himself, 'The ten-man game doesn't seem to have worked, let's use our backs.' The match took on the same glitter of the 1973 classic and although in the past there has never been what could really be called a 'Twickenham roar', it had one now.

A carefree exchange of passes had the previously wasted Duckham all set for a try, if the ball had not been directed to his feet instead of his hands. From the line-out that followed, it went right along the Barbarians' back line to Irvine, who had made himself an extra wing outside Gerald Davies. He kicked high to the New Zealand line. Batty and Karam failed to control the bounce. Mervyn Davies, who had played a great game throughout, was up to join the scramble, pick up the ball and, half-tackled, got it left-handed over the line.

This try, to bring the teams level at 13-all, was greeted with what one rugby writer described as 'an orgasm of emotion' from the crowd. I had certainly never before heard or seen such an enraptured outburst of yelling, screaming and waving of arms at a Twickenham bursting at the seams. Had Irvine goaled the conversion, for a Baa-baa win, heaven alone knows how busy the St John's Ambulance men would have been coping with split eardrums. In the event, he did not, which one must admit was only fair, since it would have been a sensational but unmerited victory.

Final score: Barbarians 13, All Blacks 13.

Chapter 24

Why Aren't They the Same at Home?

When the Rugby Football Union celebrated its centenary in the 1970–1 season the numerous special events were climaxed by a match between England and the President's XV at Twickenham on 17 April 1971. Since the visitors were the cream of overseas rugby, with the presence of such as Meads and Kirkpatrick, Marais and Du Preez, Maso, Villepreux and Dawie de Villiers, it was not surprising that England went down to the tune of 28–11. But nobody really minded about that, since it was festival rugby, highlighted by the spectacular performance of the New Zealand winger Bryan Williams, who ran in three tries.

What England supporters were rather unhappy about was that in that centenary year their side did not rise to the occasion in their regular International matches. Holders of the wooden spoon from the previous season, they did little better in 1970–1, merely a win over Ireland and a draw with France making them a poor third behind Wales who were in devastating Grand Slam mood.

Had it not been for Bob Hiller, England's entry into the 1970s would have been even more dismal.

England's solitary International win in the 1969–70 season had been entirely the doing of Hiller in a match that Twickhamists will always remember. His victims were Ireland and in that game on 14 February 1970, which was given that touch of novelty by the emergence from retirement of a portly Tony O'Reilly, the men in green were clearly the dominant force. Changing over at half-time with a lead of 3–0 from a Kiernan penalty, it seemed just a matter of time before they would pile up a comfortable winning margin. But sadly for them Hiller decided to have one of his sensational days. With England looking quite incapable of recording any sort of score, the ball came back to Hiller just inside the Irish half near touch. He essayed a drop at goal and over it went. Annoying enough to the Irish for England

Typical hell-for-leather dash by Andy Ripley, on his day one of the greatest crowd-pleasers of the England forwards of the 1970s.

to manage 3–3 quite against the run of play but worse – for them – was to follow. Just a few minutes later Hiller received again at practically the same spot and once more he tried a drop. This time it was even more of a cloud-scraper than the previous one, sailing straight and true high up between the posts.

Nobody who saw the brace of Hiller drop-kicks will ever forget them. The Irish were completely demoralised. Shackleton went in for a try, 9–3, and England had achieved their one and only success of the season.

Poor Ireland. If that was not enough, when they met again in the 1970–1 International they were beaten by Hiller again – Ireland 6 (from two tries), England 9 (three Hiller penalties). And the only other measure of success England had in the Championship in that centenary season was a 14–14 draw with France, entirely engineered by Hiller, his 14-point contribution coming from three penalties, a try and a conversion.

If ever there was a one-man band it was England that season. The unsuccessful side (apart from Hiller) was made up basically of Hiller himself at full-back; Janion, Spencer, Wardlow and Duckham the three-quarters; Cowman and Jacko Page; and the forwards Stevens, Pullin, Cotton, Larter, Ralston, Bucknall, Neary, Dixon.

Hiller withdrew from big-time rugby in the following season but Ripley and Uttley joined the forwards as regulars and if England were now without their most colourful, and helpful, full-back for many a year they at least had a pack to be proud of. It was without question the best in the Home Unions, as evidenced by the fact that when the Lions selectors chose the side to visit South Africa in 1974 they all but picked the England pack *in toto*. Cotton, Burton, Ralston, Uttley, Neary and Ripley made the trip.

So as the 1970s advanced, with England fronted by the outstanding set of forwards in the Championship, all seemed set for Twickenham to become the focal point of a winning side for the first time since way back in 1963. After all, had it not been said (and proved) by the All Blacks and the Springboks for so long that if you have forward domination you have the basic ingredient for success?

But no. In the phrase current at the time, England just could not put it together.

There was weakness at half-back. Alan Old emerged as a fly-half of some stature but nobody had come along to establish himself as a reliable permanent scrum-half. Who would be England's full-back seemed to be a matter of conjecture from match to match. There were some good three-quarters – Squires, Preece, Evans, Warfield – but the one of real world class, David Duckham, appeared to be slowly

Fran Cotton, acknowledged choice for any World XV as a prop, and appointed England captain in the 1974–5 season.

dying of starvation through the selectors' persistence in playing him on the wing.

It just did not seem to work – a great pack backed by chopped-and-changed outsides who could not consistently maintain a high standard. And the wooden spoon was England's again in 1974. And in 1975!

Yet, in the early 1970s England had done something which none of the other Home Countries had ever been able to achieve. When Wales, Scotland and Ireland had undertaken tours to South Africa and New Zealand they had always been unsuccessful in their efforts to beat the Springboks or the All Blacks on home territory. In 1972 England, under the captaincy of John Pullin, went to South Africa and not only completed their short, seven-match tour unbeaten, but included in their victories was a magnificent 18–9 win over South Africa in the single Test. In the following year they went to New Zealand, again with Pullin as leader, and after losing the first of their four scheduled matches it seemed that their South African success had been a flash in the pan. But in the final match, the Test against New Zealand, they recorded a magnificent 16–10 victory.

It was a great, history-making double. Their supporters looked forward hopefully to their reproducing the same sort of form, consistently, in the Home Internationals at headquarters – at Twickenham.